PRACE FOR A

There will come a time in our lives when all that we know to be true about our paths—our knowledge, our senses of self, our understanding of the world around us, and the part that we may or may not decide to play in the liberatory remaking of the shared communities we inhabit—will be shifted by Spirit, which might move in our lives as if it is a gust of wind or a passing breeze. Jones's *A Sacred Storm* is a gorgeous and insightful peek into the workings of the Spirit in his life—an expressive sociocultural and theological remix of the normative notions of the proverbial "storms" that tend to be understood as deterrents. Jones offers a reframe, however. Storms, whether in the realm of the personal, social, political, communal, or institutional, can also be that which orders all things to move in the direction of the divine. And it is one that buzzes with memory and wisdom. It is a book that we need now and in the days to come.

—DARNELL L. MOORE
*No Ashes in the Fire: Coming of Age Black & Free in America*

What the Rev. Dr. Christopher Michael Jones has written for us is powerfully lyrical as he weaves a metaphor of wind and storm into a melody of story and insight through the territory of his personal story and call into the preaching profession, the biblical narratives, and the history of homiletics. His ability to deftly weave these pieces together will draw you in, and his questions will push you to examine the way preaching can be disruptive and life changing. It will leave you wanting to find your footing and voice in the winds of change. I highly recommend this book for clergy and lay people alike.

—REV. VALERIE BRIDGEMAN, PhD,
*Dean, vice president of Academic Affairs, and associate professor of
Homiletics & Hebrew Bible, Methodist Theological School in Ohio*

There are certain stories that seem so unbelievable that they seemingly defy logic and possibility, that can only be explained through the miraculous power of God. Such is the story of my friend and brother, Dr. Christopher Michael Jones. In his new book, *A Sacred Storm*, Dr. Jones shares the improbable journey from acclaimed hip-hop producer who has worked with some of the industry's icons and legends to the call of God upon his life that radically shifted him to now be a pastor of a prominent church in New Jersey. Dr. Jones skillfully weaves the various biblical narratives that center "sacred" disruptions and his life, which provide the reader with revelatory insights and providential principles to simply "trust the process." I highly recommend *A Sacred Storm* to anyone who is trying to discern divine disruptions and is open to allowing the "sails" of personal destiny and purpose to be positively impacted by the "contrary winds" of a divinely directed life.

—CHARLES E. GOODMAN JR., PHD
*Tabernacle Baptist Church, Augusta, GA*

The Reverend Dr. Christopher Michael Jones in his latest work, *A Sacred Storm*, speaks to us pointedly about the significance of divine visitation and the blessing of "radical disruption" for "transcendent purposes." Like the Protestant reformer Martin Luther, whose heart was "strangely warmed," and Saul of Tarsus, who was converted on the Damascus Road, Dr. Jones also shares the impact of his own transformational experience with what he describes as a "divine disruption." We are so forever grateful for this seminal text, which reminds us that God still speaks. God still troubles the water. God still visits us in the night, and God still speaks through the still small voice and the wind. Thankfully, the life-altering wind that Dr. Jones began to feel in the studio in the late fall of 1996 is blowing today. That wind remains evident in his preaching, teaching, parenting, marriage, and pastoral ministry. I am blessed to be not only his pastor and father-in-faith, but his brother and his friend. I encourage everyone in the hip-hop community, church, university, seminary, corporate and nonprofit sector to stop what you are doing and read and be blessed richly by this historical work. Indeed, *A Sacred Storm* will change your life!

—BISHOP DONALD HILLIARD JR., D. MIN.
*Cathedral International, Perth Amboy, New Jersey*

This book offers insight into the spiritual journey of one of the leading minds of our time. The Rev. Dr. Christopher Michael Jones' path from hip-hop to ministry is nothing short of amazing. I am certain that readers of all ages and vocations will be greatly inspired by this phenomenal text.

—BISHOP H. CURTIS DOUGLAS
*Presiding prelate, Covenant Fellowship Alliance,*
*Dabar Bethlehem Cathedral*

The Rev. Dr. Christopher Michael Jones' monumental, compelling weave of autobiography, history, and practical theology doesn't skip a beat. It is a stellar must-read. You will be emboldened to join generations of "prayerful morally courageous" folk who with God's anchoring presence navigated the worst of storms with indelible impact.

—Dr. Bernadette Glover
*St. Paul Baptist Church, Montclair, NJ*

Many theologians struggle to express their conversion or embrace of faith without rejecting the culture that influenced them before they met Jesus. Often, the church emphasizes separating from the world, overlooking the connection between Jesus's earthly parables and our relationships with God, humanity, and the world. Reverend Dr. Christopher Michael Jones is brilliant at bridging this gap. *A Sacred Storm* immerses the reader in his world in the 1990s, balancing his role as a music producer with rap icons like Biggie Smalls and pop stars like Janet Jackson. Yet, it was Jesus Christ who captured his heart, and now he uses his life experiences with both the Lord and the music industry to lead souls to God. A must-read for those seeking to encounter God in the everyday spaces around them and in the music that shaped them.

—Rev. Nicole Duncan-Smith
*Journalist, Advisory Board member at the Hip-Hop Museum,
and host of the Sunday School Dropout*

Former hip-hop producer, now pastor-theologian, Christopher Michael Jones, takes us on an existential and musical journey that reveals it is possible to meet the Holy through hip-hop. As readers turn the pages, they will hear the magisterial names of the musical industry, but amid those names, there is a resounding name that rings out clearly—Jesus! Jones reveals and testifies that the windy storms of life might ultimately be a sacred breeze of the divine. This book will take you behind the scenes of the hip-hop industry, but more than that, it will leave you with a sense of hope in God.

—The Rev. Dr. Luke A. Powery
*Dean of Duke University Chapel and professor of Homiletics and
African and African American Studies, Duke Divinity School/Trinity
College of Arts & Sciences*

While many books examine the deep connections between religious experience and the phenomenon of hip-hop, it is incredibly rare to have these issues engaged by someone with an elegant and expansive theological perspective and the experience of playing an influential role in the development of hip-hop. This is the uniqueness provided by Dr. Christopher Michael Jones. The result is an extensive work that plumbs the depths of both the Christian experience and the hip-hop culture to offer extraordinary insights that will be meaningful to anyone seeking to better understand the rich capacity of this musical genre and its artists to articulate deeply religious concerns. After reading this work, one is left with a more complete understanding of how God has continued to speak to God's creation through the voices of those who may live outside the walls of the church and yet illuminate the fundamental hope of the gospel story.

—David Latimore, PhD
*Director of Betsey Stockton Center for Black Church Studies,*
*Princeton Theological Seminary*

A SACRED STORM

# A SACRED STORM

*When God Speaks through Radical Disruption*

## CHRISTOPHER MICHAEL JONES

the pilgrim press

The Pilgrim Press, 1300 East 9th Street
Cleveland, Ohio 44114
thepilgrimpress.com

Published 2024.

Printed on acid-free paper.

Scripture quotations, unless otherwise noted, are from the New Revised Standard Version of the Bible, © 1989 by the Division of Christian Education of the National Council of the Churches of Christ in the United States of America, and are used by permission. Changes have been made for inclusivity.

Library of Congress Cataloging-in-Publication Data on file.
LCCN: 2024930931

ISBN 978-0-8298-0082-1 (paper)
ISBN 978-0-8298-0083-8 (ebook)

Printed in The United States of America.

# Contents

# PROLOGUE

As I stood directly in front of the nine-foot stainless steel and bronze sculpture of the lyrical genius Christopher "The Notorious B.I.G." Wallace, also known as Biggie Smalls, I became overwhelmed with feelings of awe, deep appreciation, and a sense of fulfillment. It was 81 degrees outside, and the sun radiated with the gaze of a proud mother looking earnestly upon the brilliance of her own children. Tourists from across the globe strolled back and forth across the Brooklyn Bridge. Standing in front of me were two onlookers taking pictures of this brilliant work of art properly entitled "Sky's the Limit in the County of Kings, A Tribute to the Notorious B.I.G." I absorbed each recognizable distinction: the ebony skin, the bronze crown, the Coogi sweater mosaic, the tiger medallions, and the golden heart and microphone held in each hand.

I was pulled back to a time when Black youth and young adults like Biggie and I expressed our creative genius through a cultural movement that arose out of the ashes of poverty. To us, hip-hop was the church. The MC was the preacher. The DJ was the worship host. The B-Boys, break-dancers, and pop-lockers were the liturgical dancers. The journalists and graffiti artists were the scribes. The concert arena was a sanctuary. The bodies who danced to rhythmic anthems of classics like "La Di Da Di," "Oh, My God!" "I Know You Got Soul," and "Fight the Power" were its members.

Our call-and-response tradition was firmly established in vocal expressions like "Ayo!" and "Word!" rather than "Amen" or "Hallelujah!" Much like the church, our gatherings were spiritual, sacred, and rooted in an authentic search for a sense of belonging. Hip-hop as a cultural movement and musical art form gave us hope in the midst of great pain and suffering. We were in search of community and some resemblance of transcendent hope. We understood DJ Kool Herc's 1973 clarion call emanating from two turntables, a breakbeat, and a microphone at Sedgwick Avenue in the Bronx to be our own distinct form of worship. For the emerging hip-hop generation fighting to belong in urban landscapes across America, we believed God was with us—but God's liberating presence needed to be experienced in a new and authentically different way.

Was it only yesterday that I stepped outside of the Marriott Marquis Hotel, the site of the 1993 Jack The Rapper "Family Affair" convention in Atlanta, and found myself swept away by a swarm of Bad Boy Entertainment street promoters? Members of the Bad Boy entourage were handing out makeshift McDonald's burger containers emblazoned with Bad Boy's famous insignia advertising their "B.I.G. Mack" campaign and announcing the launch of Sean "Puffy" Combs's (aka P. Diddy) new record label. There were promotional CDs featuring Craig Mack's Grammy-nominated single "Flava in Ya Ear" and menus of Biggie's soon-to-be-released debut album *Ready to Die*. At the center of the crowd, embodying the elements of a West African coronation, stood P. Diddy, Craig Mack, and Biggie. Their grand entrance at the Family Affair represented a changing of the guard within the recording industry. Bad Boy Entertainment had arrived, and a new sound was taking over.

Only two years later at the Source Awards held at the Paramount Theater in Madison Square Garden, I sat approximately fifteen rows away from the podium when The Notorious B.I.G. received his award for "New Artist of the Year." This particular Source Awards ceremony would go down in history as the day when the private riff between Bad Boy Entertainment and Death Row Records became a public spectacle. After Death Row

Records CEO Suge Knight mounted the stage with recording artist Danny Boy to receive his award for "Best Motion Picture Soundtrack," Knight dissed Bad Boy Entertainment's CEO P. Diddy. Amid boos and jeers from a predominately New York City–laden crowd, Knight announced for all the world to hear, "Any artist out there that wants to be an artist or stay a star—and don't want to worry about an executive producer trying to be all in the videos, all on the records, dancing—come to Death Row!"

The following year, Biggie and I were at the home estate and recording studio of NBA Hall of Famer Shaquille O'Neal. At the request of Shaq, Biggie and I had been flown to Orlando to record what would become arguably the most acclaimed collaboration between an NBA superstar and a hip-hop icon. The song "Still Can't Stop the Reign" was produced while Shaq was in hard-fought negotiations with the Orlando Magic and Biggie was still recovering from the sting of Tupac Shakur's diss record "Hit 'Em Up." "Still Can't Stop the Reign" featured samples from British R&B group Loose Ends' 1987 hit single "You Can't Stop the Rain" as well as audio of a rainstorm in South Africa. As the record's producer, I believed the storm captured the frustrations of an emerging hip-hop generation struggling to find its voice on the backend of the Gulf war, a death-dealing recession, the brutalization of Rodney King, the O. J. Simpson acquittal, mass incarceration of Black bodies, the Million Man March, federal government shutdowns, and the "War on Drugs" campaign—all of which affected Black and Brown communities disproportionately. The original sample pointed to the inevitable storms of the human experience. In their lyrically reflexive responses, Shaq and Biggie suggested to us that, while such storms are common, all storms ultimately come to an end. During a time of personal struggle and social challenge, both artists rewrote their own narratives to point toward a better future in which they intended to, eventually, reign.

By early 1997, Biggie shared with me his intent to co-write and co-executive produce the next album for the rap group Salt-N-Pepa. Biggie came up with the idea of using a sample from Sting's classic hit, "Shape of My Heart." (The rapper Nas later used the same sample for his single, "The Message.") The second sample Biggie wanted to use would be extracted from Minnie Ripperton's "Inside My Love." He requested that I produce both songs for the newest Salt-N-Pepa project. We jokingly argued over the phone as to whether the concepts Biggie created for Salt-N-Pepa would fit the distinct sound I was trying to establish as an emerging producer. Biggie called frequently from his home in Teaneck, New Jersey, to persuade me: "You can do this, playboy!" The very last time I spoke with Biggie was in late February 1997. His life was taken the next month in Los Angeles on March 9.

The book you hold in your hand offers insights on what I believe to be hip-hop's contribution to conversations normally held in the church and academia, including discussions on how communities take shape, how religious belief systems are formed, and how such belief systems are always subject to change. It wrestles with questions related to the meaning and function of faith in the life of a believer. It is also the result of twenty-five years of reflecting on my own conversion experience—an unexpected and holy storm that radically intruded upon my career as a multiplatinum hip-hop and R&B record producer. This book reflects my understanding of how the unexpected storms we experience in life can point us toward a more meaningful and deeper relationship with God.

I have experienced life with two feet fully planted in secular society, and as a seasoned pastor and trained theologian in the church. The need for belonging is innate in us, whether we have been raised outside of the church or within it. How we find our place of belonging is greatly contingent upon how our communities value our humanity. In many regards, hip-hop has embraced the marginalized and oppressed in ways the church has not. I pray that this project adds to the greater discussions being held on matters related to how faith is currently expressing itself through mediums and within communities ordinarily not considered to be religious. And not only that: It is my prayer that these musings will encourage the heart of the reader who is struggling in a storm of their own. Please know that I am praying for you, and I remain confident in believing that God is with you and intends to bring you through your storm to the other side.

# I

# A SACRED STORM

*Immediately he made his disciples get into the boat
and go on ahead to the other side, to Bethsaida, while
he dismissed the crowd. After saying farewell to
them, he went up on the mountain to pray.*

**—Mark 6:45–46**

I t was April of 1996, and I was sitting in a private recording studio with one sound engineer and arguably two of the most famous people in the world. Shaq paced the floor intently as he listened to the playback of what we had just recorded. Biggie sat next to me listening to the same track with quiet confidence. I was the music producer of this recording, and that year I was already creating a buzz within the record industry. Record labels across the country were beginning to ask: Who is Chris Large? Who is his manager? Did you hear the song "Still Can't Stop the Reign" featuring Shaquille O'Neal and The Notorious B.I.G.? How can we get him to work with our artists?

Sitting next to Biggie, the thought didn't escape me that I was benefitting from a once-in-a-lifetime opportunity. As a result of my friend Craig "Clean Cut" Williams playing the instrumental track while riding with Shaq in his Superman truck, I was now listening to that same track being played back in a studio at Shaq's private estate. I pinched my arm just to convince myself it was really happening. Other hip-hop and R&B icons were also there—Jay-Z, DJ Quik, Rakim, Bobby Brown, Ralph Tresvant, Fat Joe, Rodney "Darkchild" Jerkins, Easy Mo Bee, Junior M.A.F.I.A., Peter Gunz and Lord Tariq, Trackmasters, and others. By July of 1996, members of the USA Olympic men's basketball team began to show up at Shaq's estate, dropping by the studio whenever their training schedule allowed to mix and mingle with Shaq's guests, who just happened to be some of the Olympians' favorite music producers and recording artists at that time.

I still remember looping a spontaneous ad-lib Biggie made in our first recording session between takes: "Can't stop . . . won't stop." Unbeknownst to any of us, the phrase "Can't stop . . . won't stop" would eventually become a global moniker and hashtag. Puffy would become famously known for coining the phrase "I thought I told you that we won't stop . . . I thought I told you that we won't stop" after hearing the unmixed version of my recording session with Biggie and Shaq. Biggie's adlib "Can't stop . . . won't stop" was exported to R&B group 112's remix "Only You," where it took on a life of its own within the broader hip-hop culture.

Those days in Orlando were unreal. In between recording sessions, Shaq treated Biggie, members from Junior M.A.F.I.A., Clean Cut, and me to courtside VIP seats to watch the Orlando Magic pummel the Detroit Pistons in the first round of the 1996 NBA playoffs. Biggie and I sat together heckling Joe Dumars and Allan Houston. We jeered Grant Hill and Lindsey Hunter. At the same time, we shouted out Shaq, Dennis Scott, Penny Hardaway, and the rest of the Orlando Magic. Following the game, we traveled with members of the Magic to a local nightclub. It just so happened that a former high school friend of mine was working security at the club when I arrived in one of Shaq's limos. This wasn't just hip-hop history. The convergence of hip-hop music with the NBA was American history; I was bearing witness to—and playing a central part in—a major moment within a cultural art form that was growing by the second.

Toward the conclusion of my recording sessions with Shaq and Biggie, I received a phone call from Perspective Records' hip-hop recording artist Pudgee the Phat Bastard. Pudgee was famously known for his first highly acclaimed single, "Checkin' Out the Ave," on Giant Records. Now working on his second album with Perspective Records, Pudgee requested that I jump on a flight as soon as I could and return to New York City to record a remix to Pudgee's new single, "Money Don't Make the World Stop." I had attended the video shoot of the original version of this same composition where I was fortunate enough to meet the legendary rapper Big L. My remix with Pudgee would include D-Nice, an original member of the rap group Boogie Down Productions, whom the world would later come to know as its favorite virtual DJ during the COVID-19 pandemic. Along with Pudgee, Relativity Records' hip-hop group M.O.P., Funkmaster Flex from Hot 97, and Blunt Recordings' hip-hop lyricist Royal Flush would also be featured.

I initially did not want to leave Orlando. For one, I took a liking to Shaq, and I could tell that he and his immediate family were being impacted by the turbulent negotiations with the Orlando Magic. The front office of the Magic franchise severely underwhelmed Shaq with their first contract extension offer. Shaq had already demonstrated the potential to be the greatest NBA center of all time, but there was a contingent of executives both in NBA circles and corporate America who held to the opinion that Shaq overestimated his market value. It became very apparent to those of us who were a part of Shaq's camp during the spring and summer of 1996 that members of his fan base in Orlando were beginning to reverse their loyalties. His mother received death threats from anonymous callers.

I also did not like the thought of leaving Orlando because Biggie and I had hit it off, so much so that Biggie openly shared with me his concerns regarding his publishing and financial status with Bad Boy Entertainment. Contrary to popular opinion, Biggie expressed a fondness toward the creative staff at Bad Boy Entertainment; he respected Puff's marketing genius and loved him like a brother. However, by the summer of 1996,

Biggie was seriously considering other opportunities through which he could express himself more broadly as an artist and a writer while also establishing himself as a formidable record company executive. The creation of Junior M.A.F.I.A., developing Lil' Kim, and inspiring other artists like Cam'ron, Lil' Cease, Mase, and Charli Baltimore were strategic moves that Biggie made to further establish his footprint as a top-tier music mogul. It was commonly understood within the recording industry that Biggie did not control the majority of his publishing rights, therefore he needed to develop his own talent and business ventures outside the reach of Bad Boy Entertainment to establish new streams of income. He shared these concerns with me, Clean Cut, and Shaq as we recorded.

While in Orlando, Biggie was noticeably affected by Tupac's diss record, "Hit 'Em Up." This testostero-centric diss record is infamously known as one of the most vitriolic diss tracks of all time. Tupac released "Hit 'Em Up" in the attempt to challenge Biggie's reign as the king of hip-hop lyricism. Allegedly, the track was heavily influenced by Tupac's misguided assumption that Biggie played a role in the violent assault against Tupac at Quad Studios in November of 1994. Within a year of the release of "Hit 'Em Up," both Tupac and Biggie tragically lost their lives over a manufactured beef between Death Row Records and Bad Boy Entertainment. This beef was marketed by national publications like *Vibe* and *The Source*, which suggested West Coast hip-hop artists were at war with East Coast hip-hop artists. Corporations within the recording industry made profits in the billions from this fabricated war. This fictitious propaganda led to the death of two of hip-hop's greatest rappers, and, as a consequence, the era of conscious rap came to a dramatic close, further establishing the birth of gangster rap as a legitimized subgenre within the hip-hop movement.

In a way, Shaq's home became a therapeutic oasis for those of us who were processing some of the common struggles often associated with acquiring overnight success in an unforgiving industry. Even the rapper Rakim joined us at Shaq's estate in Orlando to break away from his recent creative differences with Dr. Dre and Aftermath Records. The rapper Peter

Gunz also joined us after being released from prison. There were other unsung rappers, producers, and managers seeking refuge at Shaq's estate. Rakim, the "God M.C.," was gracious and kind to all of us while he himself sought rest and a sense of redirection under the care of Shaq. With Pudgee's request for my return to New York City, I was torn. I did not want to leave the safe confines of Shaq's compound—truthfully, none of us felt comfortable departing. During the mid-1990s, hip-hop created spaces for Timberland booted, gold-chain-wearing, fast-car-driving, dice-rolling young artists and producers like me who were simply looking to experience a sense of belonging in spaces much like other religious communities.

## A GENTLE BREEZE BEGAN TO BLOW

Boarding the plane at Orlando International Airport, I sat by the window in first class. Looking outside, I suddenly became awestruck by the stunning effect of the early afternoon sun. For the first time that I could ever remember, I felt an awareness of what I would eventually come to know as grace. In the simplest of terms, grace can be defined as the spontaneous God-given gift of unmerited favor. From a secular perspective, grace can be defined as a proactive acceptance, unrestricted love, and generous caring for human beings as well as oneself. Grand Puba of the rap group Brand Nubian alluded to this sense of grace in the hit song "Feel So Good" when he suggested knowledge of self should only lead to the uplifting of others. Christians believe grace to be the vehicle through which God's affirming presence and divine influence operates in the life of a believer. Grace affords a person the ability to both deepen their relationship with God and affirm the humanity of their neighbor.

Startled by this conscious awareness as I sat on the plane, I became overwhelmed with feelings of inadequacy. I recognized within myself the emotions John Newtown describes in his classic hymn "Amazing Grace." An unfamiliar sense of joy and otherworldly goodness had suddenly been bestowed upon me. The quality of this goodness—this sense that I was truly alive—could not be defined in material, philosophical, or logical terms. I sensed that I did not deserve to feel the inexplicable joy I felt at that moment. Flying north and watching the yellowish-red sunset, with highlights of violet and blue dancing upon the crowns of the clouds that remained in the sky, tears began to fall. I felt the goodness of God similar to what Moses experienced in Exodus 33:19, when God promised to "make all my goodness" pass before Moses. Although I could not quite articulate what I was experiencing in that moment, I felt suddenly that fame, fortune, and wealth no longer mattered. Becoming a famous hip-hop producer was inconsequential. At the young age of twenty-four, I recognized that an awareness and acknowledgement of God's goodness and mercy was missing from my life. This absence could not be filled with the accoutrements of fame, power, or wealth.

After reflecting deeply upon what I was sensing internally, I attempted to collect myself as best I could. I looked up at the vent just above my head to turn off the air I felt blowing. Surprisingly, the air vent was off. I looked to my left to see if the person sitting next to me had their air vent open. Their vent was also turned off. I asked the flight attendant, "Is there a draft coming into the cabin? I feel a slight breeze, and I want to cut it off."

"I'm sorry, sir," she responded. "There isn't a breeze coming into this cabin. Perhaps your air vent is on? If not, maybe you're beginning to succumb to a cold of some sort. Do you feel ill?"

In my mind, I questioned her response. "Maybe I am beginning to succumb to something? I've been in Orlando for almost a month now. I can't recall the weather ever dipping below 80 degrees while I've been here. I can't be sick. I just feel a slight breeze and want to know where it's coming from."

Upon landing at Newark International Airport, I jumped into the car service provided by Perspective Records and decided to take a quick trip to my townhouse in Jersey City. As we merged onto the New Jersey Turnpike, I asked the limousine driver, "Do you mind turning the air off?"

"Off?" he asked. "It's 90 degrees today, and the weather forecasters have said the humidity will climb as high as 80 percent. Are you sure you don't want me to turn the air on? Are you coming down with something?"

Again, my sarcastic thoughts returned. "I'm not coming down with anything. I just want this breeze to go away."

## A GENTLE BREEZE AT HOREB

The prophet Elijah emerged among the people of ancient Israel at a time when the land was divided into two kingdoms: the kingdom of Judah in the south and the kingdom of Israel (also called the Kingdom of the Ten Tribes) in the north. In those days, King Ahab, accompanied by his Phoenician wife Jezebel, sat on the throne of Israel and allowed Baal worship to take root in the northern territory. Elijah confronted Ahab repeatedly, warning him that he was leading the Ten Tribes astray. The indecisiveness of Ahab, coupled with the ill-informed allegiances of the Ten Tribes, led to the people's complacency, mounting greed, increased suffering, and spiritual disconnect from God. The kingdom of Israel was politically and economically fragmented, and the people were disloyal to their divine deliverer Yahweh, the God of their ancestors Abraham, Isaac, and Jacob.

A severe drought in the land symbolized the impoverished spiritual state of Israel. The confrontation between Elijah and King Ahab culminated in a showdown at Mount Carmel where Elijah defeated the false prophets and priests of Baal with divine assistance from Yahweh (1 Kings 18:20–40). After building an altar with twelve stones and laying on it pieces of wood dressed with cut pieces from a bull, Elijah had the people douse the altar with water before praying for God to consume the altar with fire. God responded to Elijah's prayer by sending fire from heaven, which engulfed the offering, wood, and stones. Then Elijah instructed the people of Israel to put the false prophets and priests of Baal to death. Following this event, God ended the drought and sent rain upon the land.

Unfortunately, Elijah's victory at Mount Carmel did not diffuse his struggles with Ahab and Jezebel. To the contrary, after hearing how Elijah killed all the prophets of Baal with the sword, Jezebel sent a messenger to Elijah promising to take his life within twenty-four hours (1 Kings 19:1–18). One can only imagine how psychologically, emotionally, and physically tattered Elijah must have felt. He had just defeated the false prophets of

Baal, and in less than a day Jezebel threatened to kill him. The prophet became desperately afraid, knowing Jezebel was as committed to killing Elijah as he was to loving Yahweh, and he ran away into the wilderness. There, Elijah sat down under a solitary broom tree and began to count the sacrifices he had made in the attempt to reestablish the worship of Yahweh in Israel. Overwhelmed by feelings of deep depression, despair, and despondency, Elijah asked God to take his life. How often have people fallen into the depths of despair when faced with unexpected crises that are beyond their control!

No sooner had Elijah fallen asleep from exhaustion than he was suddenly awakened by an angel and instructed to get up and eat. God intervened on behalf of Elijah, who was suffering from acute exhaustion, extreme hunger, and thirst. Elijah ate and drank, and, after laying down a second time, was touched by the angel and encouraged to eat and drink again. The angel of God shared with Elijah that the prophetic mantle he carried was too great a burden to bear. Elijah would need to be more intentional about practicing acts of self-care if he intended to finish the prophetic work for which he had been called. Elijah then traveled for forty days and forty nights to Horeb, the mount of God, where he found himself a cave and fell asleep.

It was at Horeb that Elijah experienced a personal, life-altering encounter with God. Elijah was awakened by the word of the Lord in the form of a question: "What are you doing here, Elijah?" (1 Kings 19:9). Elijah explained that he had failed in his ministerial calling as a prophet and that he could not find a reason to continue in light of his most recent confrontation with Ahab and Jezebel. He was worn down by a defiant people who refused to follow God's commandments. Elijah mourned the fact that Jezebel was successful in killing the true prophets of Yahweh; now she had her sights set on Elijah. Elijah gave in to self-loathing and fear. Perpetual fatigue, personal frustration, and feelings of absolute failure had altered Elijah's idea of success to such a degree that he had lost sight of the faithfulness of God. How ironic for one called to be God's messenger. In a moment of weakness, Elijah failed to remember how

God had already delivered him from his greatest adversaries. Adding insult to injury, Elijah assumed he was the first and the last to lead God's prophetic ministry. He felt there was no one left to carry on in the soul-draining work that he thought he alone had established as God's faithful prophet. Elijah's feelings of failure intensified. He wanted to give up and throw in the towel. He could not see a way out of the despair that had engulfed him in the middle of the wilderness.

Understanding the depth of Elijah's despondency, God instructed Elijah to come out of the cave and stand on the mountain. Standing there, Elijah experienced a theophany. The presence of God showed up in a tangible form to remind Elijah that God had not forsaken or abandoned him. In fact, God had been with Elijah every step of his prophetic journey. Yahweh was not the kind of god who called someone to a task and then abandoned them midway. The same God who called would be the God who delivered. At Horeb, God shook Elijah with a tearing wind, a ground-breaking earthquake, and a burning flame to alert Elijah that something significant was going to happen. Then after the preamble of awesome natural phenomena, God spoke from within a still, quiet breeze in the form of a gentle whisper. "What are you doing here, Elijah?" (1 Kings 19:11–13).

As tumultuous as Elijah's circumstances appeared to be, God's plans for Elijah's life were still unfolding. Elijah could not detect or properly interpret the purpose of the Yahweh's presence while lying under a broom tree or hiding in the dark cave. Elijah's assurance of divine direction came through a gracious act of God given at a moment of spiritual wrestling. In the grace of a still, calm voice—an unexplainable breeze couched in a pocket of silence—Elijah found meaning, a renewed sense of purpose, and divine direction.

## THE BREEZE TURNS INTO A GALE FORCE WIND

Changing my clothes quickly, I ran back out of my townhouse and into the same limousine that had picked me up at Newark International Airport, ready to head into downtown Manhattan. In my hand were floppy disks containing the percussion sounds and structural format for remixing Pudgee's new single. Platinum Island Recording Studios was the place to be that hot summer night. In the room were some of hip-hop's most celebrated recording artists and radio personalities: Funk-master Flex, M.O.P., my friend and acclaimed producer Spyderman (co-producer of R&B group BBD's hit "Poison"), Pudgee, Royal Flush and members of his entourage from Queens, D-Nice, and a host of other observers and media personalities. You could feel the energy permeating the space. I distinctly remember hearing the remix of Junior Mafia's single "Get Money" featuring Biggie, Lil' Cease, and Lil' Kim blearing over the studio monitors.

Still I could feel the quiet cool breeze that first visited me on the plane from Orlando. Since I had already asked two people earlier in the day if they felt this same inescapable flow of air, I dared not ask those who assembled in the recording session at Platinum Island. After all, I did not feel frigid or uncomfortable per se. The breeze felt as if someone was breathing on me with a scentless breath. No matter the course and direction of my steps, someone was traveling with me, someone whom I could not see. I knew I was not alone. Someone recorded a video of this specific studio session and posted it on YouTube. In it, I can be seen pacing back and forth on the left side of the studio. One could easily assume that I am pacing back and forth because of the intensity of the recording session. In fact, I am pacing back and forth because of the heightened awareness that someone or something was with me, putting me on edge.

At the conclusion of our six-hour recording session, I received a phone call from the head of A&R at Perspective Records, the record company launched in 1991 by Jimmy Jam and Terry Lewis—arguably the best musical production duo in the history of music. Jam and Lewis produced renowned recording artists like the S.O.S. Band, New Edition, Johnny Gill, Michael Jackson, Yolanda Adams, Usher, Alexander O'Neal, Vanessa Williams, and Mary J. Blige. Their record label called to see if I was interested in submitting instrumental tracks to their parent distribution company, A&M Records. At the time, A&M Records was preparing to solicit music for their most popular recording artist, Janet Jackson. Producers like Teddy Riley, Timbaland, and Missy Elliott were already being discussed by executives as formidable producers who would be chosen to render remixes for upcoming singles from Janet Jackson's album.

After a month of creating music in my own recording studio, I settled on seven instrumentals I believed were the best fit for Janet Jackson's forthcoming album. Instrumentals are compositions formatted in a distinct sequence that fit the three-minute time slot allowed for public radio airplay. Instrumentals rarely include an accompanying set of lyrics; a designated songwriter for a record will craft lyrics to complement the instrumental that has been created and submitted by the music producer. After the lyrics are written, typically a singer will record a demo vocal performance that captures the general mood of the song in order to give the featured recording artist a feel of the song being constructed. In some instances, the recording artist themselves will write and perform the lyrics to the producer's instrumental, making for a much easier creative process. Artists like Prince, Alicia Keys, Beyoncé, Elton John, Kanye West, Stevie Wonder, Pharrell Williams, and Bruno Mars can do all three: write, produce, and perform a music composition.

As I recorded the final instrumental onto the cassette tape that would be sent overnight express to A&M Records, I began to fall asleep. I was hungry and tired from brainstorming in my studio for over a month. I had made a desperate effort toward creating a new sound that I felt would appeal to Janet Jackson and her handlers at A&M Records, but it was a long shot. Nevertheless, I was encouraged by the invitation to submit my material.

As I fell asleep, I noticed the cool, subtle breeze that had accompanied me since leaving Orlando. Suddenly, it intensified like a gale force wind. I woke up immediately, assuming I had left the windows open, only to have the raging wind abruptly cease—just like for Elijah in the wilderness. The time was 12:01 A.M. The mystifying stillness I found myself in truly set the stage for an unexpected vision. I was nearing a Horeb moment of my own.

If you were to ask me to describe the person who suddenly appeared in my recording studio, I would labor to do so. I still struggle to describe his physical appearance, although I've pondered this matter for more than twenty-five years. The person appeared to be wearing a burgundy robe with a golden sash across his chest. A description of his complexion and hair texture escapes me. The best I can articulate is that his hair radiated like a calm fire. His eyes shone in the same manner. The only biblical reference I have to affirm what I saw and experienced that early morning is John's revelation, where we find a description of the one who stands in a blood-soaked robe among the golden lampstands and whose name is called "the Word of God" (Revelation 19:13). In his majestic presence, in the midst of the quiet stillness that settled over my private studio after the wind subsided, "Am I going to die?" were the only words I could muster.

"No, not yet," he responded. "But will you come and follow me?"

## THE GIFT OF A RADICAL DISRUPTION

The Bible gives multiple examples of what I call "radical disruptions." These are moments when God disrupts the trajectory of a person's life for the sake of fulfilling a more transcendent purpose. The Apostle Paul experienced a radical disruption on the Damascus Road while traveling to fulfill his obligation as an official arresting officer sanctioned by the religious elite in Jerusalem (Acts 9:1–9). The intent of Paul (called Saul at the time) was to stamp out a new movement that was known as the Way. Members of the Way were the disciples of Jesus who had dispersed to multiple cities after suffering persecution in Jerusalem. Paul requested official letters from the Sanhedrin to be presented at the synagogues of Damascus in order to secure their support in his efforts to arrest fugitives of the Way in their city.

As Paul approached the gates of Damascus, a great light from heaven suddenly flashed around him. The light was so radically disruptive that it stopped Paul in his tracks and enveloped his accompanying caravan. At the sight of the light, Paul fell to his knees in a reaction similar to that of others recorded in the Old Testament.

Then a voice came from heaven, "Saul, Saul, why do you persecute me?"

Paul answered, "Who are you, Lord?" suggesting he had not yet become acquainted with Jesus but understood he was being visited by a divine presence.

Paul learned quickly that Jesus was the one who visited him on the Damascus Road. The purpose of Jesus's visitation was not only to disrupt Paul's original plan but to redirect his steps for a new purpose. Paul's companions later served as authenticators of his encounter with Jesus on the Damascus Road, and thus refuted any claims that attempted to dismiss Paul's experience as nothing more than some subjective internal psychic construct.

The prophet Isaiah gave an account of his own radically disruptive experience around the year 742 BCE, the end of the fifty-two-year reign of King Uzziah. During the beginning of the westward expansion of the Assyrian empire, which threatened Jerusalem at a time when its citizens had become unfaithful to God, Isaiah had a vision of Yahweh sitting on a heavenly throne. Isaiah's vision unveiled the consequences of Israel's trivial attitude toward the holiness of God. Doom would soon come to the land at the expense of Israel's peace and prosperity. Yet the vision also revealed God's intent to redeem the wayward nation through acts of cleansing and restoration. Convicted by the vision, Isaiah left behind the safety of his family heritage and identity, and he took on the role of a servant-leader who spoke under the authority of God's divine throne.

The Reverend Dr. Gardner C. Taylor, former pastor of the Concord Baptist Church in Brooklyn and arguably the greatest orator produced by the American Christian church in the twentieth century, spoke often of the radically intrusive moment that changed the course of his life. Dr. Taylor desired to go to law school and become a criminal lawyer. One fateful night, shortly before leaving home to go to college, Dr. Taylor was involved in a tragic car crash in rural Louisiana. Another vehicle cut across his path, and Dr. Taylor collided with the car—leading to the deaths of the two white male passengers. The only witnesses to the accident were a white farmer and a white oil refinery worker. Dr. Taylor, being a young Black man in the segregated South, immediately feared that the testimony of the two white witnesses would lead to his death. By the providence of God, the witnesses told the truth concerning the awful incident. Dr. Taylor called this life-altering moment a "surprise of God's grace."[1] This radical intrusion became the defining moment through which Dr. Taylor's plans were altered irreversibly, and he was subsequently redirected to fulfill a more transcendent purpose.

In Sarah Hopkins Bradford's biography *Harriet, The Moses of Her People: A Biography of Harriet Tubman*, the account is given of the incident in which Harriet was ordered to restrain an enslaved man. Upon Harriet's refusal, the overseer took a two-pound iron weight and hurled it at the slave, but it fell short and hit Harriet in the head instead. The weight cracked Harriet's skull, causing her to suffer agonizing headaches and seizures. In addition, Harriett began to experience radically intrusive visions while falling asleep mid-sentence. In the visions, she saw herself leading slaves from their quarters in the South to freedom and safety in the North. The visions intruded on her life in such a way that Harriett felt compelled to act. Her redirected steps undoubtedly fulfilled a transcendent purpose, aiding others to freedom from chattel slavery along the eastern Maryland shore.

## A SACRED STORM

Mark's Gospel gives an account of Jesus feeding five thousand people who gathered to hear his teachings and possibly witness (or receive) one of his supernatural miracles (Mark 6:30–44). By this point in his ministry, Jesus was known for several supernatural events and had distinguished himself as a man of great compassion. Every miracle affirmed his identity as a faithful supplier of divine resources to those in need. Mark's record of Jesus showing compassion to the five thousand is no exception. (In fact, Mark says more accurately that five thousand men were fed—their

---

1. Edward Gilbreath, "Pulpit King Gardner Taylor Dies at 96," *Christianity Today*, December 11, 1995.

women and children were not included in the head count—so the crowd was likely much larger.) As the day of teaching and ministering to the crowd grew late, Jesus's disciples asked him to send the people away to neighboring villages where they could purchase something to eat. Jesus insisted the disciples reconsider their suggestion and challenged them to feed those gathered.

Forgetting Jesus's authority in the natural world and forgetting that he had already fed a similar crowd of four thousand (Matthew 15:32–39), the disciples retorted they did not have the financial means to feed so many people. But Jesus took the five loaves and two fish the disciples had within their possession, looked up to heaven, offered a prayer, and then miraculously began to break the meager supply into multiple pieces—enough to feed everyone. Mark's Gospel wants the reader to know that the people who gathered on the grassy knoll not only received their portion but were adequately filled by supernatural abundance. To Mark, Jesus represented God's fullness for a land suffering under oppression in a spiritual wilderness.

Immediately following the massive food distribution, Jesus instructed the disciples to jump into a boat, cross the Sea of Galilee, and make their way toward the village of Bethsaida. Jesus dismissed the crowds who gathered and then walked toward a nearby hill where he could pray. Prayer was not a formality or a rote practice for Jesus. It underscored his unwavering commitment to remain in intimate communion with God. Through prayer, Jesus remained centered in the ministry and purpose for which he had been sent. As the night deepened, a sudden gale force wind arose on the sea, turning the disciples' boat in a different direction, and they strained to rotate the oars in the face of this unexpected storm. According to Mark, Jesus watched the disciples struggle from his place of prayer. Then he proceeded to walk upon the surface of the Sea of Galilee toward them. Unfortunately, the disoriented disciples had succumbed to the paralyzing grip of fear and did not recognize Jesus as he approached the boat. Sensing their feelings of powerlessness, Jesus calmed the disciples by identifying himself: "Take courage! It is I. Don't be afraid" (Mark 6:50). Jesus entered the boat, and the raging winds suddenly ceased.

The significance of the unexpected gale may not be obvious until one pays close attention to where the disciples finally landed: Gennesaret. The disciples never made it to their intended destination of Bethsaida. The intensity of the storm completely altered the direction of the boat, causing the disciples to land in a location fifteen miles west of the village they initially set out to reach. The sacred storm that the disciples experienced on the Sea of Galilee profoundly changed their direction; it was a radical disruption in ways least expected.

Storms come to us in many forms and arise in both the natural order and the spiritual realm. In sacred storms, a person discerns that God is authentically present in the midst of the storm. For some, encountering God while suffering from an unexpected illness or the consequence of a poor decision is a sacred storm. For others, encountering God while navigating an untimely job termination or an abrupt separation from a spouse is a sacred storm. Still others describe surviving a cataclysmic natural event as a sacred storm in which they encounter God. In *Exodus Preaching: Crafting Sermons About Justice and Hope*, Dr. Kenyatta R. Gilbert describes the sacred as one's acquiescence to the "realities of God" and the inherent truths revealed through which such realities are experienced.[2] Our sacred storms teach us about our finiteness and God's limitless power. It is God's presence in the storm that gives us strength and assurance through the unknown.

No matter where or how one's storms arise, God uses such events to teach us about God's unending faithfulness and our need for total reliance upon God. Even in moments of great struggle, we have access to God's divine presence. We need that holy presence not only to guide us through life's stormy weather but also to teach us life lessons that await us on the other side of our temporal struggles. In the case of the

---

2. Kenyatta R. Gilbert, *Exodus Preaching: Crafting Sermons About Justice and Hope* (Nashville: Abingdon 2018).

storm that arose on the Sea of Galilee, Mark's Gospel shows that Jesus valiantly chose to venture into the storm to remind the disciples that Yahweh, the great "I Am," was with them. Jesus modeled for the disciples, and us, how faith-filled leadership ought to look when the faith of a team, family, church, or community implodes when facing adverse conditions.

## THE STORMS WE FACE NOW

Cultivating a faith and an assurance in God's divine presence amid uncertainty could not come at a more urgent time. The global coronavirus pandemic upended the lives of many and caused entire nations to reconsider their essential functions and tools for daily living. The horror of COVID-19 rose in waves as deaths started to be recorded. By early March 2020, the region where I currently pastor experienced firsthand COVID-19's death-dealing effects. Several doctors, nurses, and health practitioners in my congregation gave explicit details of hospitals quartering off their facilities and creating make-shift morgues to house the bodies of those who succumbed to the virus. Underserved communities in New Jersey (where I now pastor) and elsewhere were bludgeoned by the effects of a global storm, as COVID-19 tore the bandage off a sore waiting to burst. While more privileged communities endured more comfortably, most who lived life on the margins of society suffered dearly. In an article published that year in *The Atlantic* entitled "The Relentlessness of Black Grief," Marissa Evans wrote of Black communities being trapped in a perpetual bereavement crisis without having the privilege to stop and address the pain they feel.[3] Feelings of deep grief caused by the loss of loved ones, mixed with anxiety caused by a fear of the unknown, provoked many to wrestle with epistemological questions concerning what is actually true amid so much uncertainty.

The same dynamics stormed through the church. No one saw this pandemic coming. I cannot recall any pulpit in America predicting that

---

3. Melissa Evans, "The Relentlessness of Black Grief," *Atlantic*, September 27, 2020, https://www.theatlantic.com/ideas/archive/2020/09/relentlessness-black-grief/616511/.

COVID-19 would show up on America's shores as unexpectedly as it did. Life in the United States and in the pews has been irreversibly altered, now some three years later. While the threat of new variants has subsided to some degree, the populations most acquainted with coronavirus-related deaths continue to live in fear. Black churches especially are confronted with the reality that many of their members live in a daily cycle of perpetual trauma. Many are still grappling with the grief of their loved ones' deaths. There are parents sitting in our pews gripped with numbness from the loss of their child in the pandemic. So many are questioning whether God exists at all.

In addition to the death-dealing realities of the COVID-19 pandemic and the volatile normalcy of postquarantine life, our nation continues to fracture from a battering of political storms. Ultraconservative politicians continue to hype the fear of critical race theory in classrooms. Gun lobbyists work overtime in the shadows, enticing votes against stricter gun reform laws. Women's rights to self-agency are constantly being attacked. The crisis of contaminated water in cities like Flint, Michigan, remains unsolved and microplastics permeate the environment. Mass shootings continue to soar, and the murder rate in underserved communities remains unchecked.

America is being assaulted by multiple storms that appear to be colliding simultaneously. As fatal drug overdose rates continue to climb and academic performances among our youth within urban centers across the country continue to decline, one could argue that America's historical trajectory has been thrown in a direction we never expected and have yet to understand. Believers, atheists, and agnostics alike are actively wrestling with what it means to be fully human and engaged in community more authentically. In our social and spiritual spaces, we need discerning voices that can trace the presence of the divine in such stormy weather as well as transformational leadership that can help us navigate the storms until turbulent winds subside. We need to discern anew where God is present, how we can best care for the souls of others, how we can meet the needs of those whose lives are most radically disrupted by America's storminess, and what life-sustaining methods we can employ to strengthen our families and communities. It will take courageous inter-generational leadership and collaboration to carve a path forward as we seek understanding in the current disrupted reality we struggle to define.

For those of us who are Christian and working in leadership roles, reframing what it means to be a part of a resurrection community remains an ongoing task. Life after a storm can be a resurrection, if first there are prophetic voices who can speak to the wind with such authority that the demonic forces clutching us by the throat will loosen their grip so we can breathe. If Jesus had not joined the disciples in the midst of their struggle, the boat would have capsized and the disciples would have been lost forever. Faith and leadership matter when unexpected storms arise. We need to consider how we intend to hold to God's unchanging hand while we make sense of the modern turbulence that challenges our faith at its core.

## I NEVER KNEW WHAT HIT ME

The morning after the radically intrusive vision I experienced in my studio, I called my father to share what I had witnessed. I was adamant to him that someone whom I did not know visited me, but I knew I needed to find out their identity. At the conclusion of our conversation, my father recommended that I schedule a meeting with his pastor, the Reverend Dr. Suzan Johnson Cook. Dr. Cook had recently started a new church plant in the Bronx, after having served with distinction as the first female senior pastor of Mariners' Temple Baptist Church in downtown Manhattan. Dr. Cook was and still is a trailblazer with tremendous leader-ship gifts. Within five years of my conversion experience into the Chris-tian faith, Dr. Cook would ascend to become the first female clergyperson to serve as president of the Hampton Ministers' Conference. She would later be called upon to serve as US Ambassador-at-Large for International Religious Freedom under President Barack Obama's administration. If anyone could help me interpret my theophany, just like Elijah at Mt. Horeb, Dr. Cook would be the perfect person to offer pastoral counsel.

If anyone could make sense of the radical interruption experienced on my own Damascus Road, it would most definitely be her.

When we finally met, I proceeded to describe in passionate detail how certain I was concerning my life's purpose and trajectory. I made it clear that I was a very successful record producer and had no intention of leaving the recording industry. I explained that I was gaining a reputation as one of the industry's hottest new producers. In a span of three short years, I had already produced platinum artists like Nas, The Notorious B.I.G., Shaquille O'Neal, Whodini, SWV, Toni Braxton, and others; I contributed to four major movie soundtracks; I was preparing to launch my own music production company; I secured my own record label. I was hoping to earn a Grammy within the next five years. I never anticipated that one unexpected radically intrusive event could literally turn my life upside down, but my Horeb experience was putting my plans into question. So I asked Dr. Cook what I needed to know: "Who was the person who visited me the other night?"

Dr. Cook's response sealed the premonitions I had already been wrestling with and fighting against deep within my heart.

"Christopher, based upon what you've shared and the description you've given concerning the person who visited you in your studio, I believe you experienced an authentic call experience with Jesus. I advise you to stop everything. Reconsider your priorities. Have you thought about finishing up your college degree? I think you should strongly reconsider getting back into college, attending a credible seminary, and beginning to explore more deeply the reasons why Jesus visited you in such a powerful and intimate way. This type of visitation experience isn't common. Take a moment to pray about it. In fact, let's pray together while you are here. Let's ask God for clarity concerning the new direction God has chosen for your life."

I left her office not knowing what my next step would be. I was totally confused. Much like the disciples who experienced the unexpected tumultuous winds in the middle of the Sea of Galilee, I felt powerless.

My pager and cell phone were constantly buzzing because I had not submitted my instrumentals to Janet Jackson. In addition, I was still contractually obligated to finish the records I had already started with three other recording artists. I scheduled a sit-down with the staff at Flavor Unit Management—an offshoot of Queen Latifah's multimedia empire Flavor Unit Entertainment. I explained to my manager at the time, Shirley Bell, that something had drastically changed in my life, something truly disruptive. I didn't know what hit me, but I knew that this was a sacred storm. Surprisingly, my manager at Flavor Unit was understanding of the information I shared. "If you don't mind," she said, "I would like to pray with you also." Not only was my manager a Christian, but it just so happened that my label mate, Bryce, from Groove Theory, had also endured a recent conversion experience of his own. Shirley Bell had become quite adept at praying for mega music producers in the midst of their holy disruptions.

Several weeks later, I drove to the Bronx in my brand-new eggshell-colored Toyota 4-Runner. Lil' Kim's hit single "Crush on You" was blasting through my custom-fit 15-inch woofers. I did not waste time finding a parking space. I drove up in front of the museum Dr. Cook's Bronx Christian Fellowship Church occupied at the time, and I turned on the hazard lights. As I rushed into the museum, the Bible study had just ended with an invitation to discipleship. Dr. Cook asked, "Is there anyone here tonight who would like to start a new life with Jesus?"

I don't remember what else was said. I just walked down the aisle, eyes filled with tears, wearing a motorcycle jacket with Karl Kani jeans and two gaudy gold chains. I had $3,500 in my pocket that night. I slammed the money at the altar, fell on my knees with my arms stretched wide, and cried, "Jesus save me!" My life had been radically disrupted, tossed like a boat on the Sea of Galilee. I did not fear the future, for I knew Jesus was with me. Even without the certainty of my life's direction, I understood that with God I could face whatever awaited me on the other side of my sacred storm.

## A SACRED STORM AROSE IN MONTGOMERY

History records one of America's greatest prophets emerging not by choice, but through what I have already described as a sacred storm. The Reverend Dr. Martin Luther King, Jr. was a twenty-six-year-old minister— just a year into his pastorate at the historic Dexter Avenue Baptist Church in Montgomery, Alabama—when, on December 1, 1955, a middle-aged woman named Rosa Parks got arrested for refusing to give up her seat to a white passenger on a Montgomery city bus. Rosa Parks did not choose her seat randomly. To the contrary, she, along with other courageous Black women of the civil rights movement, deliberately chose prophetic defiance in the collective attempt to dislodge a system of racial oppression. In the days immediately following Parks's arrest, mass meetings were organized in Montgomery churches, including Dexter Avenue Baptist Church where Dr. King was pastor, and the Montgomery Improvement Association was formed. To Dr. King's surprise, the members of the newly formed MIA elected Dr. King to serve as their first president. Dr. King later wrote in his autobiography that his first response to being selected was a fifteen-minute panic attack. King did not expect to be pulled into leadership to navigate a conflict between brooding forces and thought initially that the MIA's plans were unethical and possibly unchristian. It was not until Dr. King found comfort through prayer and counsel from his wife, Coretta Scott King, that he relented, surmising that perhaps God was in the midst of the unexpected storm that showed up in Dexter Avenue Baptist Church on December 5, 1955.

Mark's Gospel makes it clear that, when Jesus recognized the disciples' struggle within the storm, he joined them. No matter how hard the raging winds blew, nothing could have separated Jesus from the disciples whom he so deeply loved. The sacred storm would become a platform through which Jesus could teach the disciples and us about God's character and infinite goodness, even and especially in the midst of radical disruption. God was with them as much as God is with us now. It is true, the disciples' plans abruptly shifted, much like the plans of the prophet Isaiah, the Apostle Paul, and Dr. King. However, Mark's Gospel affirms that, no matter how volatile the change, Jesus journeyed with them toward the unexpected path that lay ahead.

## EXPERIENCING RESURRECTION IN A STORM

It can be argued that the storm on the Sea of Galilee was a preamble to the storm that landed on the day of Jesus's crucifixion. Jesus's state-sanctioned crucifixion on a hill called Golgotha challenged the disciples' faith. They had been accommodating of a Messiah they presumed would be enthroned like the kingly messianic figures from Israel's past; they did not know how to respond to a Messiah who had been crucified. In the intensity of that storm on Golgatha, the disciples did not understand that the lessons learned on the Sea of Galilee would prepare them for a new life with the resurrected Jesus on the other side of Calvary. Empowered by the Holy Spirit, however, the disciples reclaimed the lessons learned in the sacred storm: lesson about the gift of radical disruption, the value of unwavering faith, confidence in the shared life of community, and the anchor planted in the resurrection hope of God dwelling among them. No matter how intense their future storms, the great "I Am" promised to be with them no matter where the winds of struggle would take them.

The disciples also remembered the leadership that Jesus modeled on the boat, grounded in the spiritual disciplines of prayer, reflection, service, and proclamation. Jesus displayed the power of selfless leadership, a willingness to set aside one's own narrow interests for the sake of working together for what James MacGregor Burns defined as "transcending goals."[4] Jesus's concern for the well-being of the disciples was unshaken by the threat of the gale force winds that made travel practically impossible. Without the presence of strong, compassionate, caring leadership, it is practically impossible to break through a storm. Strong leadership will always be needed to weather the struggles of human experience—and not merely leadership in action, but leadership in faith

---

4. James MacGregor Burns, *Transforming Leadership* (New York: Grove Press, 2003).

through which action is sustainable. As used by the Black women who organized the Montgomery Bus Boycott of 1955, this God-centered leadership requires learning how to factor in the inevitability of unexpected storms while charting a course toward freedom, justice, community, and, for people of faith, communion with God. Jesus was an innovator in radically disrupted—and radically disruptive—leadership, and innovation is required of us as we continue to make sense of life in the aftermath of seemingly constant and volatile disruptions. This type of faith looks beyond the storm, toward a God who promises to lead us to our purpose along the adjacent shore.

## I DON'T KNOW WHERE I'M GOING BUT THAT'S OKAY

After the midweek Bible study ended at the Bronx Christian Fellowship Church, I was immediately surrounded by church members who welcomed me into their spiritual family. They could not have known the consequences of my decision to accept the call to discipleship extended by Dr. Cook that night. Representatives from Perspective Records were calling my phone, asking for the instrumentals I had promised I would submit to Janet Jackson. Nas, whom I had produced previously, was beginning preproduction for his new album, *It Is Written*; it was a foregone conclusion that I would participate in his new album since I produced the song "One on One." I was also in the studio finishing up a remix with RCA's hot R&B group SWV. My handlers were urging me to submit records to Jay-Z, who had already started preproduction on his forthcoming album, *In My Lifetime, Vol. 1*. Life was busy, and new contract proposals were being presented almost daily. I was getting anxious at the thought of missed opportunities now that my life was changing so quickly.

Ultimately, nothing else mattered. My life had been radically disrupted. The cool breeze that followed me from Orlando to Newark International Airport to Platinum Island Recording Studios in New York City, and eventually to my own private studio in Jersey City, gave way to a calming peace as Jesus made himself known to me on the night of my conversion experience. I thought about the purpose of the wind that followed me, and I realized that the Holy Spirit had been preparing me in advance for the one who would show up in my studio at 12:01 A.M. Once I yielded fully to Christ's invitation to serve him, my new journey began and turned in a direction I never anticipated. "No going back now," I thought.

I called my entertainment lawyer, Scott Felcher, Esq., and informed him that I was done with the recording industry. I called my management team at Flavor Unit and shared the same. There would be no more records coming from Chris Large for the time being.

"Chris, what are you going to do?" my attorney asked in disbelief. "Where are you going to go? How are you going to make a living?"

"I don't know where I'm going," I responded, "but that's okay. It doesn't really matter. I know who is with me. That's all that matters now."

# 2

## LEADING INTO THE WIND

*When evening came, the boat was out on the sea,
and he was alone on the land. When he saw that they
were straining at the oars against an adverse wind,
he came toward them early in the morning, walking
on the sea. He intended to pass them by.*

**Mark 6:47–48**

In May of 2022, local media outlets in northern Israel reported that strong winds caused extensive and expensive damage to the tourist destination known as the Yigal Alon Promenade, on the western shore of the Sea of Galilee. The wind was so strong that sidewalks along the promenade were ripped up and fences were knocked down. Windows adorning the facades of high-end clothing stores were shattered. Footage of the storm's aftermath looked like a scene out of a Godzilla movie. In a matter of hours, winds with gusts of 86 mph had uprooted palm trees, sunk merchant boats anchored along the shore, toppled over parked cars, and dislodged several buildings from their foundation.

At 685 feet below sea level, the Sea of Galilee—called a sea according to ancient tradition—is the lowest freshwater lake on Earth and the second-lowest lake in the world after the Dead Sea, a saltwater lake. The

Jordan River flows through it, from north to south. Nazareth, where Jesus spent his boyhood years, is about twelve to fifteen miles west of the Sea of Galilee. In the warmth of spring and summer months, cold air rushing down from the hills often meets the warm air rising from the sea, causing turbulent winds to spiral in multiple directions simultaneously. At their apex, these winds turn into violent storms, causing boats to overturn and merchants to lose their lives at sea. Mark's Gospel specifies that it was evening when Jesus instructed his disciples to get into their boat—a time of day when temperatures drop sharply. When the cool winds from the hills where Jesus was praying blew over the surface of the still-warm waters, the perfect environment for a storm was created. In all likelihood, the disciples sailed into a storm similar in potency to the storm that decimated the Yigal Alon Promenade.

## STRAINING AGAINST AN ADVERSE WIND

Like any corporation that decides to change its model of operation due to volatile changes in the marketplace, I had to make critical decisions that would affect both my life and the lives of those who had become dependent upon my success. Following the encounter with Jesus in my studio, I received a phone call from Blunt Recordings' head of A&R, Bryan Leach. Bryan Leach later became the founder and CEO of Polo Grounds Music, which currently holds a roster of stellar talent, including Grammy-nominated artist A$AP Rocky, Latin Grammy award winner Pitbull, Calboy, A$AP Ferg & Jay Gwuapo, Yo Gotti, Hurricane Chris, and many others. Bryan requested my services to produce a music track for Blunt/TVT Recordings' rising superstar rapper Mic Geronimo. Mic Geronimo began to reach a crossover audience through his appearances on a reality show featured on MTV Raps. The song I was contracted to produce would eventually be named "Street Life," featuring Uptown Records' talented recording artist Monifah.

Halfway into the recording session at Platinum Island Recording Studios in Manhattan, I received a phone call from the front desk. Someone was on hold who needed to speak with me urgently. When I gave permission for the person to be given access to the studio line, I was greeted coldly.

"Why didn't you tell me that you had a recording session today?"

"Why should I have to tell you?" I responded. "You're not my manager anymore."

"This game doesn't work that way. I'll be there within an hour. When I get there, you better have 10 percent of whatever they gave you to produce that song. If you don't have my money by the time I get there, you already know what's going to happen."

Regrettably, this type of conversation is commonplace within the hip-hop and R&B recording industry—especially during the late 1980s and early to mid-1990s. Typically, when a young musical talent emerged from an impoverished urban population, the first financial backers who offered their support were members of the illegal narcotics industry. These underground urban financiers offered access to expensive musical instruments and high-quality digital recording tools, at no cost to the young talent. They flew their musical talents to music conferences and premier music award shows, where they were introduced to music executives, producers, and recording artists. New artists deemed to be an exceptional talent were given access to an apartment, a house, or a car free of charge. Daily incidentals were fully covered. They were afforded jewelry, the hottest trends in clothing, and trips to vacation destinations of their choice.

Motivating this investment from illegal narcotics entrepreneurs was the idea that the talent being supported would eventually make their breakthrough in the recording industry, creating opportunities for both themselves and those attached to them. As the talent's success in the industry grew, they were expected to hire their secret financial backers as managers. Investors-turned-managers then used the commissions from an artist's compensation to wash illegal money. In one of the more recent examples of how gang life and drug trafficking can wash money through an artist, rapper Tekashi69 (aka 6ix9ine) became infamously known for an affiliation with members of the Bloods gang, who were alleged in court to have funneled money into his fledgling career. Tekashi69's investors cleaned and recouped their illegal money by charging commissions for managerial services rendered.

In fairness to those young narcotics entrepreneurs who had little or no access to economic opportunity in the late 1980s, 1990s, and early 2000s, urban centers across the country were suffering from the reconstruction of an economic and racialized caste system in America. Political conservatives in the late 1960s and early 1970s had advocated for rigid reforms to liberal social policies viewed to grant overly generous relief for those populations trapped in America's urban centers. They believed poverty and rampant drug use to be the result of a flawed culture within urban America, rather than of structural factors related to race and class. The rhetoric of "law and order" was crafted to motivate white working-class voters who felt threatened by the sudden progress of African Americans. The conservative reforms diminished access to pertinent social services and allowed for the swift migration of corporations out of bustling metropolitan areas into the surrounding suburbs.

Blue-collar factory jobs, once plentiful in urban areas, suddenly disappeared, along with the employment opportunities they offered to their local communities.[1] The decline in urban jobs was exacerbated by technological shifts unfolding in the workplace, eliminating many opportunities available to a lower-skilled workforce. While highly educated workers benefited from changes to the job market, blue-collar workers in the inner city fell further behind. Youth and young adults who attended racially segregated, underfunded public schools and lacked a college education found themselves feeling hopeless, realizing they would no longer have access to the financial stability available to the previous generations.

Straining to find a path forward in the face of such adverse political winds, many urban youth of the Gen X and Millennial generations turned to the narcotics game to create the capital needed to find a way out of the

---

1. William Julius Wilson, *When Work Disappears: The World of the New Urban Poor* (New York: Vintage, 1997).

urban ghetto. Big-time dope dealers like the Supreme Team, Rick Ross, Michael "Harry-O" Harris, Fat Cat, Alpo, Azie Faison, and Rayful Edmond were pushing drugs to local dealers at a massive scale to finance an underground economy that emerged under the "War on Drugs" of Ronald Reagan. Youth and young adults were hounded by increasingly militarized police forces that prowled to imprison the underserved and uneducated for the slightest infraction. The protections afforded by financial independence were inaccessible to them without jobs that offered a livable wage. Def Jam Recordings founder Russell Simmons frequently spoke about these social tensions as the main motivational factor driving his pursuit to build a major hip-hop and fashion conglomerate. Russell used hip-hop as a platform to fight poverty and poor education in those communities shut out by systemic racism and low economic opportunity.

To be clear, young disadvantaged members of the urban poor were no less prideful of their intellectual prowess or inherent abilities than their white suburban counterparts. However, the generational effects of systemic racism, the impact of "Reaganomics," and a constantly shifting job marketplace severely diminished the potential for upward economic mobility. A majority of poor youth in New York City during the mid-1980s and '90s were forced to consider a few limited career paths if attending college wasn't an option. They could flock to their local park to showcase their lyrical or musical talents or take to the street corners to sell crack cocaine. Those lacking the stomach to sell drugs on the street corner could join the military and be sent to the front lines in places like Panama, Iraq, and Somalia, or take manual jobs for minimum wage in supermarkets or local warehouses if they could find one. It's no wonder that hip-hop and drug trafficking went hand in hand. For every Afrika Bambaataa or KRS-One you could find an illegal narcotics entrepreneur like a Boy George or a Pistol Pete. For every LL Cool J or Run-DMC you could find a Bimmy or a Supreme.

Attending community jams—like the famous gathering that took place at the tenement building at 1520 Sedgwick Avenue in the Bronx on August 11, 1973—was more than just a recreational gathering for young people. It was a cultural movement, a shared social outlet, as young people gathered to express their concerns for upward economic mobility and to make sense of a deep desire to belong. It was the site of a community jam that birthed hip-hop. DJ Kool Herc's signature break-style and the emergence of hip-hop artists like Run-DMC, I Fat Boys, Schoolly D, Ultramagnetic MCs, and Big Daddy Kane set the scene for a disrupted generation to voice their aspirations in their own creative way. Breakdancing, graffiti art, and the MC complemented the role of the DJ in creating an alternative sacred space for an underserved population trapped in the bowels of an unforgiving urban landscape.

## LEADING AT THE POINT OF SAIL

Navigating the wind requires a crew to be skilled and knowledgeable with their boat. A sailboat cannot make headway by sailing into the wind directly. Its movement is made possible when the sail is angled slightly toward the wind so that the streams of wind are parted by the sail unevenly, creating high and low pressure on the two sides of the sail. The sail is pulled into the low-pressure vacuum, and this force—what sailors call "sail force"—moves the boat. The direction of its movement depends upon the underwater keel of the boat, which acts in the water like the sail acts in the wind. The sail force is balanced by the keel force, propelling the boat forward.

In the instance when a boat does not have a sail, a different set of skills are required. When a boat doesn't have a sail, it can still move forward, but the crew must remember to relax. Rowing into the wind requires competent coordination: firing the right muscles at the right time while relaxing all others not involved in the movement. The skill of relaxing nonessential muscles decreases tension that could interfere with desired movement. Learning how to relax while rowing into the wind saves energy and keeps the boat from veering off course. In addition, the crew that rows into the wind without a sail must remember to stay connected, keeping the blade in the water as long as possible while pulling the oars through the "drive" phase of a set. Remaining connected to the oars with even pressure while keeping the blades in the water creates stability and speed, propelling the boat forward into the wind. When the blades are released from the water, staying connected to the oars allows for a controlled recovery before the next rowing set.

## THE VALUE OF LEADING INTO THE WIND

When an unexpected wind overcame the disciples in their boat, the disciples became frozen by fear and forgot the key tenets of navigating a boat into the wind. Either they forgot how to angle the sail or they lost their ability to relax and stay connected while rowing their oars. Mark's Gospel doesn't tell us if the boat was equipped with a sail or not, but regardless: the disciples lost their momentum. They stalled in their progress. Jesus, having assessed the stagnation of the disciples, approached the faltering crew. Their disorientation from the storm, magnified by the energy they had exhausted in their efforts to control the boat, led to a sense of hallucination. From the disciples' point of view, only a ghost could walk toward them on the water with such ease. It took Jesus seeing the disciples, assessing their struggle, and then choosing to meet them where they were—trapped in the middle of a gale force wind—before the disciples could regather their faculties and be reassured that Jesus had not abandoned them.

For Jesus, leading into the wind began with properly assessing the conditions that led to the panicked standstill of the disciples. He recognized that the disciples were overcome by nature's hindering force and in dire need of leadership. They had forgotten their own skills and the rules of sailing, frightened by circumstances they felt they could not control or handle. Therefore, Jesus made the courageous decision to walk upon the water and meet the disciples where they were, knowing how deflated they had become. It takes courage to walk in the direction most would walk away from. Without courage, one cannot lead into the wind to uplift those who struggle in the middle of a storm.

It can be argued that, in many regards, the Christian church in America today appears to be flailing with its spiritual oars much in the same way the disciples appeared to be flailing in the middle of the Sea of Galilee. And it is not just the Christian church. Corporations, governments, educational systems, and sociopolitical structures are also flailing their moral, ideological, and philosophical oars in the unexpected storm now commonly known as the postquarantine era. But it is more than the winds of the COVID-19 pandemic that caused spiritual stagnation and a lack of innovative thought both in the church and the marketplace. Political unrest, ecological injustice, police brutality and mass incarceration, unbridled racism, international wars played out on the lands of the Middle East, inadequate social systems for healthcare and education, and general social discord have all contributed to the storms of destabilization.

Sounding the alarm and raising our collective consciousness, Dr. Marvin A. McMickle argues in *Where Have All the Prophets Gone? Reclaiming Prophetic Preaching in America*, "In the face of all that is currently happening in our world, it is shocking to note that the voice of the prophet is too rarely heard."[2] To the detriment of the moral authority of many pulpits in America, the prophetic voice has become mute at a time when the church should be leading the charge in calling for lamentation, repentance, reparations, and robust initiatives to uplift the least fortunate. We need to lead into the wind with radical efforts that build up economic empowerment, improve our mental health, increase adequate housing, provide a livable wage, better educate our young people, and take a more holistic approach in reteaching America how to engage in compassionate acts of kindness—especially toward the most vulnerable in our local communities. We need more prophets and more truth-tellers, more hope dealers and sage thinkers.

Hip-hop has its own prophetic illuminators, like KRS-One, Chuck D, Common, Lauryn Hill, Nas, and Rakim. Lyricists like Melle Mel,

---

2. Marvin A. McMickle, *Where Have All the Prophets Gone? Reclaiming Prophetic Preaching in America* (Cleveland, OH: Pilgrim Press, 2006), 6.

Prodigy, Joey Bada$$, Mos Def, Talib Kweli, De La Soul, Ice Cube, Black Star, Donald Glover, Black Thought, Sister Souljah, Dead Prez, and Queen Latifah spoke to the social ills and injustices that often restricted the flow of life and access to urban communities so desperately in need of care. Rap groups like NWA, Public Enemy, Brand Nubian, Goodie Mob, Boogie Down Productions, Da Lench Mob, I Roots, X-Clan, Jungle Brothers, and Grandmaster Flash and the Furious Five all spoke through a prophetic lens when critiquing the systemic injustices commonly experienced in their cultural context. Both the church and hip-hop need proclaimers, mystics, and provocateurs who are not afraid to assess the storm and then speak the truth to a world firmly entrenched in its appeasement of corrupt powers at the expense of the poor and oppressed. Such prophets need to "see" much in the way Jesus "saw" the disciples straining with their boat in the face of an adverse wind, in the way rapper Tupac Amaru Shakur "saw" the plight of young Black males in the inner city and wrote to the pain of those who would never live long enough to mature beyond an immature "thug life" in the 'hood. It is through such clarity that a leader can assess the most appropriate methods to rescue and redirect those who have become stagnant under the hard press of a disruptive storm. Leadership begins with the clear recognition of variables at work in turbulent circumstances that are dimly lit to others. Wise seers not only discern the direction the wind is blowing, they walk in that direction—all the while keeping their gaze upon the discouraged until the discouraged recognize they are not alone.

## ONE OF THREE CHOICES

When I hung up the phone at Platinum Island Recording Studios, I was faced with one of three choices. I could call my recently hired management representative at Flavor Unit Entertainment for reinforcements. I could solicit Mic Geronimo's support by having him call his enforcers out of Flushing, Queens. Or I could find a local bank and withdraw the 10 percent being demanded by this former co-manager, illegal narcotics entrepreneur, and music financier. Doing the latter could increase the odds of avoiding a potentially violent outbreak in the middle of a major recording session. Resisting could lead to the irreversible harm of those I felt responsible for in my recording session. Mic Geronimo was already navigating an internal struggle with Irv Gotti, founder and president of Murder, Inc., who at the time was lending his services as the executive producer of Mic Geronimo's latest album. Behind closed doors, Mic Geronimo and Irv Gotti split over creative differences. Soliciting enforcement from Queens or Brooklyn would only create an even greater chain of violent reactions I was not willing to provoke.

Further complicating matters, a press release had been published in Billboard that I—along with Def Jam Recordings' Redman, Erick Sermon, Montell Jordan, RCA Records' RZA (of Wu Tang fame), Columbia Records' DJ Muggs from Cypress Hills, Immortal Records' Dilated Peoples, DJ Ralph M of Funkdoobiest, Loud Records' E-Swift of Tha Alkaholiks, and Tommy Boy Records' DJ Lethal from House of Pain—agreed in principle to be managed by Buzztone Management.[3] To be mentioned in *Billboard* was a sign that a recording artist or music producer had ascended to the top of the food chain. They had arrived in the world of entertainment. This official press release signified to my former financiers once and for all that the professional side of our relationship had come to a close. While I was grateful for their initial investment to expedite my development as an emerging "super producer," their initial investment paled in comparison to the portions of my publishing rights that were secretly whittled away from the records I produced early in my producing career. The *Billboard* press release also brought heightened awareness from competing management firms and record executives in Los Angeles that felt threatened by Buzztone Entertainment's expansion in the music industry. Not too long after the *Billboard* article, rumors swirled that the owner of Buzztone Entertainment was found dazed, beaten, and covered in cigarette burns in a hotel

---

3. *Billboard*, July 29, 1995, 22.

in Long Beach, California. Reports suggested the owner allegedly claimed that amnesia prevented him from remembering who accosted him or held him against his will. No police report was filed. However, producers like myself, RZA, Redman, Erick Sermon, and others were conveniently dropped from our managerial relationship with Buzztone without explanation. It seemed the purpose of the alleged kidnapping had been to force the owner to release the producers he had recently added to his roster.

This type of violence had become commonplace within the hip-hop recording industry by the year 1995. Record companies and artists alike used violence to remove competition in their own respective niches within the growing consumer market. Rumors swirled continuously of recording artists hiring goons to threaten or shoot other upcoming artists. Some artists hired gangsters to assault record company executives accused of dealing unfair contracts or stealing publishing. Record company executives hired shooters to threaten competing executives in the attempt to corner a regional market or gain control of a talent roster. Unfortunately, given the violence against Buzztone Entertainment's owner, I would have to navigate the music industry without managerial representation for a spell.

A year, several months, and a few more recordings passed before I reconnected with a few of my early financiers. In the minds of those associated with this former management group, their relationship with Chris Large had never really ended. It was only put on hiatus out of necessity, but their tentacles remained. The threatening call to Platinum Island Recording Studios on that brisk fall night in 1996 was proof that our relationship had not changed in their minds. "When I get there, you better have 10 percent of whatever they gave you to produce that song. If you don't have my money by the time I get there, you already know what's going to happen." I could refuse to comply and by doing so, put all who participated in this recording session with Mic Geronimo and Monifah at risk. My best option would be to turn over what was being asked to avoid a potential violent outcome. Sometimes leading into the wind requires making hard decisions that benefit the whole rather than a select privileged few.

## REDIRECTING THE POWER OF SAIL FORCE

On March 30, 2023, students in Nashville, Tennessee, responded en masse to a call to action, gathering at the state capitol to protest for stricter gun control laws. Just three days earlier, six people—including three children—had been killed in a mass shooting at the Covenant School in Green Hills. It was America's 129th mass shooting of 2023 according to Gun Violence Archive, a nonprofit tracking gun violence data. On Monday, April 3, 2023, students nationwide participated in a mass walkout to demonstrate against gun violence. Feverish debates over the nation's gun laws arise regularly after mass shootings, yet Americans are divided over whether legal changes would reduce mass shootings, according to a Pew Research poll. Nearly two-thirds (65 percent) of American adults who describe their community as urban say that gun laws and gun violence are a major problem, compared with 47 percent of suburbanites and 35 percent of those who live in rural areas.[4] About half of adults (49 percent) say there would be fewer mass shootings if it was harder for people to obtain guns legally, while less than half either say this would make no difference (42 percent) or that there would be more mass shootings (9 percent).

One could argue, unfortunately, that discussions on the prevalence of mass shootings and the need for gun reform in America continue to be brushed aside by politicians. In a Gallup survey conducted in October 2023, gun owners were more likely to cite personal safety or protection as the reason they own a firearm, contrary to assumptions that Americans defend their right to bear arms because of their love for hunting or other recreational activities.[5] Although six in ten American adults identify gun

4. Katherine Schaeffer, "Key Facts about Americans and Guns," Pew Research Center, September 13, 2023, https://www.pewresearch.org/short-reads/2023/09/13/key-facts-about-americans-and-guns/.

5. "Guns," Gallup Historical Trends, https://news.gallup.com/poll/1645/guns.aspx.

violence as a huge societal issue, attitudes on the matter differ widely by education, ethnicity, age, and community affiliations, according to Pew. Sixty-four percent of women favor increased strictness in US gun laws, compared to 51 percent of men. Democrats and Democratic-leaning independents are far more likely than Republicans and GOP-leaning supporters to see gun violence as a major problem (81 percent versus 38 percent). At the core of the prevailing sail force of opinions opposed to gun reform is a disputed interpretation of the Second Amendment of the Constitution: the right to "bear arms." For lack of skilled leadership and the force of an even keel, the violent tempest of debate brings our collective boat to a standstill. To adequately address such a nuanced subject, transparent dialogue is needed—both in private and public settings.

## SAIL FORCE AND A NEED FOR MORAL COURAGE

The harnessing of sail force is what gives a craft power to move forward. The more force applied to a sail, the further and quicker a craft is propelled. The less force applied, the slower a craft is propelled. To counter the rate of propulsion, a sail must be shifted, allowing for the release of force and subsequent changing of direction or speed of the craft. Much in the same way, in order for the sail force of gun reform to move forward, there must be a shifting of ideas. As an ethical concept, the notion of "a right to bear arms" needs to be revisited and unpacked. Philosophically, one can argue that a right constitutes a "good in itself," regardless of the consequences of that right. However, one's rights must be grounded in our experience of the world. The right to bear arms cannot be considered "good in itself" or worthy of protection in the face of mass shootings like the one that took place in Nashville. With every ensuing tragedy and emerging statistic that objectively measures the harm being caused by America's resistance to gun reform legislation, the soul of American society diminishes by the day. Our collective fetishization of guns is closely aligned with our allegiance to unfettered capitalism, the myth of rugged individualism, and our worship of imperialism at the expense of the vulnerable—both domestically and abroad. We have made our "right to bear arms" a religion unto itself, replacing an authentic relationship with a God who bears life and desires to preserve life.

To shift the sails and ethically redirect the power of sail force, we need to develop moral courage. We need to allow our heightened concern and indignation to generate brave behaviors intended to confront violent societal norms. Moral courage is not to be confused with heroism or social control. Instead, moral courage is the set of ethical and/or spiritual underpinnings that nurture one's ability to confront power with truth. The morally courageous are not, and will not be, afraid to declare that gun violence is a public health crisis without geographic or socioeconomic boundaries. Those considered to be influencers within the hip-hop community must make a greater effort to denounce the element of gun violence embedded in its culture, much like Migos rapper Quavo did in advocating for gun reform on Capitol Hill after witnessing his nephew Takeoff gunned down in late 2022.

For the sail force of gun violence in America to shift, the Christian church cannot be afraid to lead into the wind boldly. Dr. Howard Thurman, the great mystic, theologian, professor, and mentor to Dr. Martin Luther King, Jr., suggested, "It cannot be denied that too often the weight of the Christian movement has been on the side of the strong and the powerful and against the weak and oppressed—this, despite the gospel."[6] American Christians need to lead with a moral courage that is willing to wrestle with more transcendent questions pertaining to when human life begins and ends. Shifting the sails requires our sage voices, our teachers, our prophets, and our community activists declaring together from the rooftops that interpretations of the Second Amendment cannot be solely rooted in what is "right," but what is "right" and "just" in the eyes of God.

Moral courage at its best considers the whole of humanity and, if need be, steps into the winds of struggle to alter the trajectory of sail

---

6. Howard Thurman, *A Strange Freedom: The Best of Howard Thurman on Religious Experience and Public Life* (New York: Beacon Press, 2014), 145.

force and reveal a new mode of being. Hip-hop in many instances has used the power of its own sail force to create opportunities for new political thought and creative expression to speak against the systemic barriers that continue to hinder life and well-being. Civic and religious leaders from the white evangelical community shouldn't be afraid to suggest that responsible gun reform will not strip an American's right to bear arms. People with moral courage should not be afraid to tell their local politicians and nationally elected officials—on both sides of the aisle—that those who cannot pass a mental health screening or who show bias toward any minority groups should not have access to powerful weaponry. Witnessing truth to power is radically disruptive; it leads into the stormy winds of social norms, dares to shift the sail, and harnesses the power of sail force to change the course of political thought.

## INTO THE WIND WITH THE WORD

Mark's Gospel makes it readily apparent to the reader that Jesus "saw" the disciples struggling at the oar from the vantage point of an elevated location. Jesus noticed from afar that the disciples were putting all of their strength into rowing directly into a head wind. Despite the valiant resolve of the disciples, their efforts were futile. Mark impresses upon the reader that, while Jesus's heart is with the disciples, he is also in prayer. Jesus made a habit of communing with God before performing supernatural acts of deliverance.

As was the case with the historical Jesus of the first century, the twenty-first-century postquarantine church must commit to the spiritual discipline of prayer for spiritual guidance, direction, and power when confronted with the violent winds of evil, greed, and deception that exist today. Jesus is recorded in all four Gospels as having offered numerous examples of his reliance upon prayer to communicate with God and center himself in what he discerned to be God's mission in the earth. No matter how intense Jesus's daily commitments became as a preacher, teacher, and justice advocate, he found the time to commune with God. Luke's Gospel records, "But he would withdraw to deserted places and pray" (Luke 5:16) The fact that Jesus prayed as often as he did should astound us for two reasons. First, Jesus was God in the flesh, and he still prayed. Second, Jesus was occupied with more ministerial tasks than any of us ever will be, yet he found time to pray.

Leading into the wind or redirecting a surging sail force requires a power greater than the force being confronted. Jesus prayed unceasingly for spiritual clarity, for the fortification of his convictions concerning the poor, the oppressed and vulnerable, and for the strength to engage in fearless transcendent acts of service that disturbed the powers of this world and turned systems of oppression on their head. When he saw the disciples struggling at the oars on the Sea of Galilee, Jesus tapped into a spiritual reservoir that had been filled through his holy communion with God. By the time early morning began to dawn, Jesus fearlessly descended from the elevated place where he had become spiritually filled and headed toward the location where the disciples were struggling. Jesus continued onto the lake empowered by God's spiritual force, defying the raging wind as well as the natural laws of gravity to encourage the disciples suffering from the throttle of the sail force.

Jesus ventured into the sacred storm that arose unexpectedly on the Sea of Galilee to remind the disciples that God was with them. Some would call this moral courage. Others would call this an example of pure faith. Jesus's transformational leadership, cultivated through an unwavering commitment to daily communion with God, enabled him to embody the living word. Jesus not only modeled how transformational leadership can function in the face of disruption; he came with a word that ultimately saved the lives of all who suffered in the oppressive force of the raging winds.

## CHOOSING TO LEAD INTO THE WIND

In 1983, A&M Records' rhythm and blues band Atlantic Starr released a soulful single entitled "Second to None." This band was known for its hits like "Always," "Secret Lovers," "Circles," and "Masterpiece." Despite being one of Atlantic Starr's lesser-known singles, "Second to None" became a popular tune to those who listened to Black radio in urban centers across the country. This mid-tempo ballad became my sample of choice in the fall of 1996, when I began to construct a music track to fit the ebb and flow of Mic Geronimo's rap cadence. I also sampled the drums and kick from the Mary Jane Girls' classic hit song, "All Night Long," produced by the legendary Rick James. This same percussion sample was used in songs like "Around the Way Girl" by LL Cool J, "Smooth Operator" by Big Daddy Kane, "Tell Me" by Groove Theory, "Can't Wait" by Redman, and "Hands on You" by Fat Joe and Dre featuring Jeremih and Bryson Tiller. To complete the construction of this soon-to-be classic hip-hop hit, my music co-collaborator—acclaimed hip-hop lyricist and friend Clean Cut—suggested that we have Monifah sing the hook from the classic soul funk hit "Street Life," released in 1979 on MCA Records and performed by the jazz fusion group The Crusaders. The Committee Music Group CEO and eventual Grammy-nominated producer/songwriter David Caton played the keys on the hook underneath Monifah's sultry voice.

The Atlantic Starr sample played in a loop on the studio monitors while I further pondered my decision. This was the fateful night when those former managers/investors discovered my location at Platinum Island Recording Studios. As I considered the potential fallout from choosing to mishandle the responsibility that comes with managing over half a billion dollars' worth of musical talent in the room, I recalled the very first private conversation I had with Dr. Suzan Johnson Cook. Dr. Cook had written a Bible verse on a sticky note and strongly urged me to keep it in my possession at all times to remind me God could handle any unexpected storms that came my way. "I can do all things through him who strengthens me," it read (Philippians 4:13). I pulled that sticky note out of my Karl Kani jean pocket and read the verse over again.

The code of the streets would suggest that one should never give in to a threat. To even mention conflict would break another code of the streets: never snitch. Instead, when confronted with exploitation or violence, the streets would argue one should fight fire with fire. If need be, hire "goons," or, as some would say, employ a "pack of wolves." A pack of wolves, however, must be fed, and wolves stay close to their food supply until that supply runs out. Hustlers and gangsters who are savvy enough to identify and invest in a recording talent are unlikely to leave such talent without forceful coercion. When threatened by wolves, conventional thinking suggests backing away slowly without making any aggressive movements to avoid being trapped or surrounded. Doing so may save your life in the wild, but never guarantees that the wolves of the street will go away. There is always the risk of agitating a wolf, as evidenced by the rapper 6ix9ine's fallen relationship with the Nine Trey Gangsta and the rapper Gunna's estranged relationship with YSL.

Feeling that cool, calm breeze with me in the studio with Mic Geronimo and Monifah that evening, I chose to lead into the wind. I felt that protecting the safety of all those in the room was of greater importance to me than choosing to protect my own ego or personal safety. To that end, I left the studio abruptly to make a cash withdrawal. I remember a white Lexus LS 400 following me to the ATM, its speakers blaring Lost Boyz' "Renee" while I walked down the street. When I returned to the studio, I was alerted by the front desk that a party had arrived to discuss a pickup. Prior to the cash exchange, I can recall praying for the first time, "Jesus, protect me and protect us." My decision to choose a nonviolent means to escape a confrontation in the studio pales in comparison to Jesus's decision to rescue his disciples on the Sea of Galilee. Yet, I believe leading into the wind requires the moral courage Jesus demonstrated on the Sea of Galilee to make tough decisions and a willingness to put the interests of another over the interests of an individual. Leading into the wind comes as the fruit of prayer, no matter how long or short one's prayer may be. Leading into the wind is a form of servant leadership that is made possible through the spiritual discipline of prayer.

## SOCIETY NEEDS LEADERS WHO LEAN INTO THE WIND

Times of crisis can prompt communities to seek a more transcendent understanding of their sense of purpose and belonging. The same is true of the church: crisis prompts an increase in prayer. Black churches, and especially those churches made up of members who've been forced to live on the margins of society, are well acquainted with the spiritual discipline of prayer. African slaves in America often risked floggings to worship God and communicate with the divine in their own native tongue. Congregations like First African Baptist Church, Bethel A.M.E., Emanuel A.M.E., and St. Bartley Primitive Baptist Church emerged in the South and provided sacred spaces in which enslaved communities gathered to hold on to hope in an acutely oppressive land.[7]

The crisis of COVID-19 increased prayer among church members, as well as those who do not affiliate with an official religion of any sort: praying for loved ones stricken by COVID-19, for those who lost businesses due to abrupt economic shifts, for relief from acute poverty, for better access to jobs, and for the curtailing of police brutality. Christians continue to pray for those who are depressed, grappling with feelings of loneliness, and struggling to find their place in a world that feels unsafe. The pandemic allowed many to come to the realization that an activity-driven life will never be as fulfilling as a life rooted in prayer. The postpandemic American church can learn much from those spiritual communities of past centuries. Robbed of their God-given freedom and sense of autonomy, enslaved African slaves rooted themselves in the spiritual, leaning into the wind toward a Savior and Redeemer they believed would rescue them from daily storms and set free those who had been held captive by the machine of chattel slavery.

As the modern church navigates new technologies, new forms of pastoral care, and new visions for how we will shape the world we live in today, we cannot forget the power of prayer. As a result of prayer, Jesus saw his disciples struggling at the oar on the Sea of Galilee. Because of prayer, Jesus found the moral courage to leave his elevated place and brave the forceful winds upon the sea to encourage his followers who

---

7. Albert J. Raboteau II, *Slave Religion: The Invisible Institution in the Antebellum South* (New York: Oxford University Press, 1978).

were disheartened for a lack of advancement. Prayer enabled Jesus to tap into a power greater than the forces that hindered their progress in the middle of the sea. Prayer propelled Jesus with enough soul-force to defy the laws of nature, reminding the disciples that God was with them and could see them through.

One of the lessons we learn from navigating through our sacred storms is that God is with us in the midst of turbulent winds that blow against our progress. Our sacred storms teach us that even in the most violent of circumstances, our God is accessible and has a word to comfort us: a holy assurance that we will not sink nor will we remain stagnant for too long. God is always working on an alternate plan. It might look different than what we expected, but the good news is that the God who sent us into our unexpected storms remains present with us and intends to direct us toward an alternative route that will work out for our good in the end.

Therefore, those of us who have been given the responsibility to lead should lead and lean into the wind with the soul-force and moral courage of a Dr. William Barber II, one of the founding coordinators of the Moral Mondays Movement. We should not be afraid to lead with the moral courage of a Sybrina Fulton, social activist and mother of the late Trayvon Martin. We cannot be afraid to lead with the moral force of a US Congresswoman Maxine Waters, the dynamic truth-teller and community servant-activist. Nor can we be afraid to lead artistically with the conviction of a Kendrick Lamar, Beyoncé, Nas, Joey Bada$$, J. Cole, Lauryn Hill, or Common or to lead creatively with the moral courage of a Ryan Coogler, Spike Lee, Oprah Winfrey, Denzel Washington, Viola Davis, or Sheryl Lee Ralph. And we cannot shun our responsibility to affirm the younger generations who have already taken the helm of moral leadership in resisting those senseless systems of oppression that strangle the life out of the most vulnerable in our communities.

Communities, grassroots organizations, and churches must be intentional about cultivating moral courage among their members and protecting their emerging leaders from the onslaught of death-dealing ideologies and traditions that quench hopes and dreams for the future.

With prayer and faith, we can change the trajectory of the winds howling over the social-political landscape of our time. Even if those winds originate from the ire of narrow-minded thinkers who oppose gun reform, equal access to an adequate education, job security, voting rights, or a fair living wage, we can, with moral courage rooted in prayer, redirect the sail force blowing against the stern of social progress.

## LEANING INTO A GREATER FORCE

"You got that for me?" he asked as I passed the envelope into his hands. He quickly surveyed who was in the studio.

"I do, actually," I replied. "In fact, I have more for you than you think. I have a prayer for you too."

When he left, I turned back toward all the brilliant talent in the room and continued the session as planned. The calm cool breeze that had followed me since my departure from the recording with Shaq and Biggie a few weeks earlier was still present with me in Platinum Island Recording Studios this particular evening. I am certain this presence, which I now know to be the Holy Spirit, gave me the moral courage to face into the wind of potential violence and choose to walk in peace. The mere presence of that greater force changed the trajectory of the storm. God was with me, as much as Jesus was with the disciples on the Sea of Galilee, and, as a result, the Holy Spirit transformed a space that could have become volatile into a space God claimed as sacred.

# 3

# THE SHOOTING AT QUAD STUDIOS AND THE GIFT OF RADICAL DISRUPTION

*But when they saw him walking on the sea, they thought it was a ghost and cried out; for they all saw him and were terrified. But immediately he spoke to them and said, "Take heart, it is I; do not be afraid."*

**—Mark 6:49–50**

In early November 1994, I had been contacted by Mercury Records' Bruce Carbone to consider producing a remix for his new hip-hop group Ill Al Skratch. At the time, Ill Al Skratch were already scorching urban radio with hit songs like "Where My Homiez (Come Around My Way)" and "I'll Take Her," featuring R&B crooner Brian McKnight. Bruce suggested to my handlers at the time that he was looking for a new sound to accompany Ill Al Skratch's soon-to-be released third single, "Chill with That." Producer Easy Mo Bee and I were contracted specifically to reconstruct the original version of the song produced by the LG Experience.

When popular hip-hop and R&B producers in the 1990s and early 2000s were contracted to remix a song, they would receive a Digital Audio

Tape (DAT) containing a recording of an original vocal performance. DATs contained a digital signal and playback medium that producers would sync up to their drum machine, sampler, or keyboard of choice. Once properly synced, the producer would reconstruct a new musical composition retaining the vocals from the original song, ultimately recording the new composition and vocals to a brand-new two-inch track tape for the record label. Once the remixed composition received final approval, the producer would render a final mixing for digital mastering, packaging, and marketing for mass distribution. Some of the greatest hip-hop and R&B remixers in the 1990s include Pete Rock, Puff, Easy Mo Bee, Teddy Riley, Dr. Dre, Jermaine Dupri, Havoc, RZA, Erick Sermon, the LG Experience, DJ Muggs, Allstar, DJ Marley Marl, Q-Tip, DJ Premier, Da Beatminerz, Kanye West, Organized Noise, Hank Shocklee, Buckwild, and Trackmasters.

Most hip-hop producers of the late 1980s, 1990s, and even the early 2000s preferred to work in a specific studio with a specific mixing console. A mixing console takes in multiple inputs from microphones, live instruments, drum samplers, digital keyboards, DJ turntables, and DATs, and merges them together so they can be sent to a set of speakers as one signal. Depending upon the make of the console, the signal being fed into the speakers offers a distinct audio sound to the producer: a warmer feel in the audio, perhaps, or a punchier boom-bap type of sound. Producers in the late 1980s and 1990s who preferred a warmer sound in their musical production often liked the Neve console. Those of us who preferred the punchier boom-bap experience often used the SSL. A producer's personal choice dictated which studio they would work out of more frequently.

**WEDNESDAY, NOVEMBER 30, 1994**

Once negotiations between my handlers and Bruce Carbone were completed, it was agreed that I would begin working with Ill Al Skratch on Tuesday and Wednesday, November 29 and 30, at Unique Recording Studios in New York City in the Theater District. Unique Recording

Studios was chosen because of its technological innovation and SSL boards.

November 30 of that year was a notable day for many reasons: The Beatles released their first album in twenty-five years, "Live at the BBC." The National Football League announced that the Jacksonville Jaguars would become the league's thirtieth franchise. Boyz II Men's hit single "I'll Make Love to You" ascended the pop charts. Shaquille O'Neal scored 41 points for the Orlando Magic against the Sacramento Kings. Mass serial killer Jeffrey Dahmer was reported to have been beaten to death at the Columbia Correctional Institution. And the Bosnian War continued to surge with casualties in Bosnia and Herzegovina. November 30 was also a significant date in hip-hop history.

Around 7:00 P.M. on November 29, I began to lay down the track for what would become the first of two versions of a remix I created to the song, "Chill with That." At a BPM (beats per minute) of 89, the studio began to sway back and forth rhythmically to a sample of the song "Angela" from Tappan Zee Records recording artist Bob James. This sample was complemented with the kick, hi-hat, and hard snare from the Honeydripper's "Impeach the President" and chopped up into a new musical cadence that fit the vocals of Ill Al Skratch. My personal guest DJ Doughboy accompanied me in the recording session, offering symbiotic DJ scratches on the track to undergird the hook:

> *"You can get with this or you can chill with that,*
> *but don't sleep on the deep type creep with my style.*
> *You can get with this as you chill with that,*
> *but don't sleep on the deep type creep with my style."*[1]

By 12:30 A.M. on November 30, I was well into the throes of mixing the complex combination of sounds pulsating out of the studio monitors when I received a call on the studio phone.

---

1. Ill Al Skratch, "Chill with That," Mercury Records, 1994.

"Hi Chris." It was the receptionist. "There are police here from the local precinct. They want to come into your session to check things out. There's been a report that Tupac just got shot, and they want to confirm whether he got shot in your recording session or if the shooting took place at Quad Studios around the corner."

My recording session at Unique Recording Studios was radically disrupted on Wednesday, November 30, 1994.

## THE GIFT OF RADICAL DISRUPTION

The genre of hip-hop is rooted in radical disruption—not only social and systemic disruption, but, I would argue, a sacred storm. Radical disruptions are sacred storms in the sense that God is actively working toward a specific purpose within and through them. These storms can be experienced through a series of historical events, relationships, prophetic protests, or similar acts of courage in the face of great challenges. Hip-hop as a cultural movement provided a vehicle for the voices of marginalized youth in urban cities across America to emerge like a storm on the Sea of Galilee. Coupled with the aggressive sound of the boom-bap and the emergence of braggadocious fashion apparel, a distinct public posture, and original slang influenced by hip-hop's most popular songs, hip-hop's prophetic voice challenged the cultural norms of a dominant society conditioned to maintain the status quo at the expense of the poor and the oppressed.

Hip-hop's sacred storms sounded like the historic recording performances of Chuck D, Flava Flav, and Public Enemy on their second album, *It Takes a Nation of Millions to Hold Us Back*, and of NWA's album *Straight Out of Compton*. Released on the heels of escalating racial violence throughout New York City in 1988, Public Enemy crafted a dense rhythmic sound that provided a sonic platform upon which the social injustices of systemic racism and police brutality could be challenged.

Often, divine intent in radical disruptions is not easily detected. If we are to believe that God works sovereignly through history, we can faithfully deduce that what seems disruptive to us may ultimately be the movement of God's will. This revelation does not come to us immediately. God's active presence in our lives seems paradoxical and, more often than not, involves a shroud of mystery. Stormy life disruptions leave us questioning God's benevolence and disoriented in our purpose. Moreover, when God disrupts our trajectory, God usually visits us through a sequence of events—one following the next, disruption following disruption. Without discernment, we are unable to detect the interweaving of God's divine activity concealed under the cloak of mystery. Nevertheless, as intrusive as God's disruptions may be, prayer and reflection allow our understanding of sacred storms to become richer and fuller over time. And as our understanding evolves, so does our relationship with the divine author of such disruptions. The fathers of the early church believed such deeper spiritual meanings concerning God's intended purpose would be revealed to us in time through the course of our own personal spiritual journey.

## DISRUPTION AT MOUNT HOREB

Exodus 3 records the great prophet Moses's career-altering encounter with God at Mount Horeb. At that time in his life, Moses was far removed from his earlier days as an Egyptian prince and his subsequent conflict with the law in Egypt. It was apparent that, should Moses ever return to Egypt, he would go as an Israelite—his ethnic identity by birth—rather than an Egyptian—his social position by adoption. During this time, Moses was employed by his priestly father-in-law, Jethro, serving in the occupation of a shepherd. While feeding Jethro's flock of sheep somewhere southwest of Midianite territory, Moses came face to face with a supernatural occurrence. God appeared in a fiery theophany to initiate a divine call to prophetic ministry for the sole purpose of delivering the Israelites from their bondage in Egypt (Exodus 3:2). Moses had no intention of taking on the responsibility of serving as a prophetic voice for Yahweh—the God of his father, the God of Abraham, Isaac, and Jacob (Exodus 3:6). Moses had grown very content with living a life of simplicity outside the margins of power in Egypt. The biblical story gives no indication that Moses intended to return to Egypt.

Nevertheless, "the angel of the Lord" appeared in a flame of fire coming out of a bush, radically disrupting Moses's own agenda of contentment. This holy alteration of Moses's life plans introduced him to a more transcendent purpose. The term used for this bush, *sĕneh*, suggests a relatively small thorny shrub. Moses would have been well acquainted with such thorny shrubs, having spent many cold nights working to keep warm in the wilderness. It was commonplace for shepherds to burn thorny shrubs for warmth and as a source of light to keep watch of predators in the wild. Moses knew they would usually expire when lit. This particular thorny shrub, however, would not expire. Instead of burning up, it burned on and on.

Understanding that this burning bush represented the divine, Moses stepped to the side to see why this particular thorny shrub had not extinguished its flame. As Moses approached the bush, God called him by name: "Moses! Moses!" (Exodus 3:4). In ancient Semitic culture, calling individuals by name repetitively was a sign of endearment. Doing so affirmed a friendship between one person and the other. Moses understood that he was being summoned by someone who intended him nothing but good. By responding ("Here I am"), Moses embraced the idea that this divine being desired his full attention (Exodus 3:4). He took off his sandals as instructed by God, in reverence before the holiness he encountered at the burning thorny bush. Mount Horeb became Yahweh's temporary abode as the presence of the Holy surrounded and disrupted Moses.

## MINISTERING TO THE RADICALLY DISRUPTED

When the COVID-19 pandemic encroached upon the tri-state area in March 2020, food insecurity in the region surged. Regional companies and local stores were closing by the day. Malls, movie theaters, and main thoroughfares were being sealed. Unemployment rates soared. Stock markets fell. Local businesses came to a screeching halt. Despite the abundance of government assistance and Paycheck Protection Program (PPP) loans, families could not keep up with the rising costs of living.

Individuals from every class bracket poured into lines where food drives were being hosted. Wherever the basic necessities for living could be found, people showed up en masse.

First Baptist Church of Hillside in Hillside, New Jersey, became one of those locations where people came to receive food, diapers, baby formula, laundry detergent, cleaning supplies, face masks, rental assistance, clothing, hygienic products, gift cards, counseling, travel assistance, and other referral services. The leadership of FBC-Hillside partnered with local politicians, corporations, nonprofits, and food banks to fight hunger, poverty, provide sanitary products for women, and host vaccine clinics. Many other churches did the same in their communities, embracing God's invitation to serve those who experienced acute suffering under the weight of the pandemic. The churches that were most prepared to serve their constituents during the pandemic were those that interpreted the disruption as a sacred storm. Prior to the pandemic's onset, churches were content with functioning as they had previously. After the onset of the pandemic, churches grappled with their methodology in response to such a radically disruptive moment. The pandemic awakened congregations to the sad reality that business could not carry on as usual. For many churches, the collision between contentment and crisis prompted the emergence of a faith and praxis that could respond to the needs of those whose lives had been shifted.

Like Moses on Mount Horeb, many professionals, volunteers, church members, and others who experienced the pandemic as a sacred awakening responded in faith with moral leadership. I am appreciative of churches and ministries like the S.I.S. (Sisters in Spirit) Ministry at First Baptist Church of Hillside, who purchased meals from local restaurants in high volume to both feed the food insecure and help sustain the bottom line of Black-owned businesses in the community. I am appreciative of churches like the Sacramento Capitol City Seventh-Day Adventist Church, led by Pastor Damian Chandler in Sacramento, who created warm stations in their sanctuaries to house the homeless during the cold of winter. I am also appreciative of online platforms like Women of Color in Ministry, led by its founder and president, Dr. Martha Simmons, and for cutting-edge communications specialists, like Dr. Timothy Farmer, who played a pivotal role in helping churches and church leaders embrace the technological shift needed to update their ministry praxis during the pandemic.

One cannot deny that the church needed to be awakened. Our American "mainline" Christian denominations are becoming increasingly irrelevant by the hour. Statistics from the Public Religion Research Institute's consolidation of 2023 census data suggest the percentage of religiously unaffiliated Americans has risen to 26.8 percent.[2] Even though the ranks of all religious Americans rose by 10.6 million believers (7 percent) from 2010 to 2020 (when the overall population grew by 7.5 percent), the number of Episcopalians and Methodists dropped by 19 percent each. The Lutherans plummeted by 25 percent. Presbyterians lost nearly 1 million members over the same period—the largest drop of the major denominations in the United States.[3] Even mainline Black churches have suffered attrition. Not only has attendance in the Black church been on the decline over the last twenty years. Dr. Brianna K. Parker notes in the 2021 Barna Group study, "Trends in the Black Church," that significant numbers of youth within the Black church have disengaged from the spiritual institution that raised Gen X and Baby Boomers.[4] Younger generations are less engaged by mainline traditional congregations with their rules about membership and doctrine. Instead, Gen Z and Millennials increasingly find faith through the exercise of

---

2. PPRI staff, "Religion and Congregations in a Time of Social and Political Upheaval," May 16, 2023, https://www.prri.org/research/religion-and-congregations-in-a-time-of-social-and-political-upheaval/.

3. "PPRI Releases Groundbreaking 2020 PPRI Census of American Religion," July 8, 2021, https://www.prri.org/press-release/prri-releases-groundbreaking-2020-census-of-american-religion/#:~:text=The%202020%20Census%20of%20American%20Religion%20includes%2013,mainline%20Protestants%2C%20Black%20Protestants%2C%20Jewish%20Americans%2C%20and%20more.

4. Brianna K. Parker, *Trends in the Black Church: Celebrating its Legacy and Investing in a Hopeful Future* (Ventura: Barna Group, 2021), 146.

deconstructing religion and dismantling the systems that perpetuate historical disadvantages.

Hip-hop, in many respects, has always offered an alternative communal experience for America's youth and young adults who are tired of the dogma taught in so many of America's Christian congregations. The radical disruption provided by hip-hop can be a sacred storm for the church, challenging congregations to rethink what it means to be in community and engaged in works of justice outside the sanctuary walls, and to reexamine the habit of overburdening youth with dogmatic teachings that neither affirm their humanity nor expand their understanding of God's love and concern for all in the communities in which they live. Whether the church's routines are shaken by a pandemic or a musical movement, God remains present. And in God's presence, we find a call to embrace a divine reorientation—discovering new modes of thinking, new ways to love more radically, and new reasons to trust God's faithfulness in life's most disruptive moments.

## DISRUPTION AT UNIQUE RECORDING STUDIOS

By November 30, 1994, Tupac Amaru Shakur, known by his stage names 2Pac and Makaveli, had become a household name to those who immersed themselves within hip-hop culture during the early 1990s. Both an artistic genius and lyrical savant, Tupac was born in New York City on June 16, 1971, to parents who were both Black Panther Party members. Tupac's mother, Afeni Shakur, was famously known for successfully defending herself in court against charges of conspiracy and attempted murder with Tupac in her womb in May 1971.[5] Not long after Afeni's acquittal, Tupac was born.

Raised as a child of the Black Panther Party and member of the Black liberation movement, Tupac would move with his mother Afeni to

---

5. Arielle G. Cribb, "Don't Ask Us about Freedom: Stories of Gender and Injustices in the Cases of Afeni Shakur, Angela Davis and Assata Shakur," thesis, Cornell University, Aug. 2009, https://ecommons.cornell.edu/bitstream/handle/1813/13786/Cribb%2c%20Arielle.pdf?sequence=1&isAllowed=y.

Baltimore in 1984 and then to the San Francisco Bay Area in 1988. By 1990, Tupac had joined the acclaimed funkadelic rap group Digital Underground as a roadie and backup dancer. Tupac drew national attention in 1991 for performing the "Humpty Dance" in a video produced to market the eponymous song. Later that year, Tupac released his first verse, "Same Song," on the Digital Underground–produced single featured on the soundtrack to the film *Nothing but Trouble*. In this same film, Tupac made his acting debut, taking a small supportive role alongside actors Dan Aykroyd, John Candy, Chevy Chase, and Demi Moore. Tupac released his debut album, 2Pacalypse Now, in November 1991, which positioned Tupac to become a central figure in West Coast hip-hop. Tupac achieved even greater success with his follow-up album, *Strictly 4 My N.I.G.G.A.Z.*, in February 1993; hit singles like "I Get Around" and "Keep Ya Head Up" propelled Tupac to multiplatinum success.

In addition to his achievements in the recording industry, Tupac continued to gain recognition for his charismatic performances on the silver screen. In 1992, Tupac starred in the urban classic *Juice* with Omar Epps, Jermaine Hopkins, and Khalil Kain. In 1993, Tupac starred alongside Janet Jackson in John Singleton's romantic classic *Poetic Justice*. During this same year, Tupac befriended Biggie Smalls, a.k.a The Notorious B.I.G., and invited Biggie to perform live at his shows. In 1994, Tupac starred in arguably his most famous role as "Birdie" in the highly acclaimed film *Above the Rim*, playing the part of a drug dealer who struggles to maintain his grip over the local community. It was heavily speculated that Tupac took on the character of a real-life drug dealer, a luminary figure who dominated a considerable portion of illegal drug-related activity within certain sections of New York City.

As mentioned previously, rarely would you find artistic talent in urban centers like New York City, Philadelphia, or Los Angeles who were not attached to some form of criminal element in the late 1980s and early 1990s. Tupac was no exception. It became commonly known to those of us in the recording industry that Tupac began to associate himself with a certain faction of individuals who were firmly in the street. These individuals were entrepreneurial in spirit; many of them possessed impeccable organizational and leadership skills. They were also quite adept at surviving the challenges of the underworld, and, if threatened in any kind of way, they would discipline you with extreme forms of violence. No matter how great the talent, not even the music industry could save us from the rules of the underworld. If you violated the codes of the streets or offended such individuals in any way, they would exact revenge against you. In the most extreme cases, they would even take a life if doing so meant they could retain their street cred.

This was exactly the case in the early morning of Wednesday, November 30, 1994. At the same time I was scheduled to remix the Ill Al Skratch single, "Chill with That," Tupac was scheduled to record a song with Uptown Records's recording artist Lil' Shawn. Tupac's session with Lil' Shawn and Groove Theory producer Bryce Wilson took place at Quad Studios, less than a city block away from where I was recording at Unique Recording Studios. Tupac was scheduled to record his song with Lil' Shawn at the request of Uptown Records founder and president Andre Harrell. The idea was to broker a new partnership with Tupac in the hope that he would consider a feature on Andre Harrell's new hit TV show "New York Undercover." Several recording artists and music executives were present at that scheduled recording, including Bad Boy Entertainment's president and founder, P-Diddy, Biggie Smalls, and members of Biggie's new rap group Junior M.A.F.I.A. In addition, there were hangers-on, spectators, and a certain caliber of entrepreneurial individuals—one of those being the manager of Lil' Shawn at the time.

Unbeknownst to the majority of those who attended his recording session that night, Tupac got into a dispute with one of those luminary street figures over the phone. Allegedly Tupac became combative while negotiating his fee of $7,500 with Lil' Shawn's manager prior to the recording session. Tupac was unaware that the individual he conflicted with over the phone had felt disrespected by the dispute and subsequently had arranged for Tupac to be robbed in the Quad Studios lobby. The assailants attacked him at gunpoint with the instruction to rob his $20,000 diamond-encrusted Rolex watch, $30,000 diamond ring, various bracelets, and gold chain. Gun shots went off, and Tupac was left bloody on the floor with members of his entourage. Reports suggested Tupac was shot in the right thigh, left hand, scrotum, and twice in the head; the Rolex was left on his wrist. Tupac and his party took the elevator upstairs and remained there until the police arrived.

Quad Studios wasn't the only place where officers from the Midtown South Precinct showed up with force that night. While mixing at the console early that Wednesday morning, detectives arrived at the door of my studio room in Unique Recording Studios. As it was explained to me, detectives from the precinct were led by anonymous sources to believe Tupac's shooters either ran toward my recording session on the ninth floor or came from my session to attack Tupac at Quad Studios. It didn't take long for me to figure out that the detectives who bombarded my recording session didn't actually believe Tupac's assailants were in my studio. Instead, Tupac's assault served as the perfect opportunity for them to search my studio room for guns or drugs under the guise of probable cause. I was then informed that, until the crime scene at Quad Studios had been processed and cleared, I would not be allowed to leave Unique Recording Studios. Although the members of my party were not directly implicated in the Tupac shooting in any way, we were treated as if we were.

## JESUS IS THE MASTER OF RADICAL DISRUPTIONS

When Jesus descended from his place of solitude onto the turbulent sea to meet the disciples in the middle of their storm, he looked upon them with the same compassion he shared during the feeding of the five thousand. Mark paints the picture of Jesus, like Yahweh referenced in Exodus 3, coming to deliver those in need, and this deliverance becomes a revelation to the disciples in their struggle. Jesus walked across the water—suspending the laws of nature—to connect with the disciples and once again grab their full attention. Jesus walked where only God can walk, on water, to demonstrate to the disciples that God alone has power over the radical disruptions that threaten to alter their course and direction. In a sense, this storm's powerful disruption—like the burning bush on Mount Horeb—was God's powerful disruption, altering the trajectory of the disciples like Moses's destination was altered by the fiery bush. When disruptions appear, in any form, everything is subject to change. Our plans, dreams, ambitions, goals, and objectives are vulnerable to unexpected forces. With our meager efforts thus exposed, we learn what the disciples learned at sea: God can do what humanity cannot do.

God's wisdom cannot be compared to earthly wisdom. Moreover, this God that Jesus embodies cannot be described by human categories nor confined by natural law. God is wholly God, wholly Other, and can never be thwarted by the violent winds that wail in our journeys. When we read Mark's Gospel from this perspective, we are comforted with the notion that the unexpected storms in our lives do not have to be feared. There is a God who has power to calm the stormy winds blowing against the core of our faith. God is able to perform wonders in the midst of our chaos and wields power to bring stability to our places of anguish and fragmentation.

Taking their diminished faith into account, Jesus reminded the disciples to "take heart, it is I; do not be afraid" (Mark 6:50). His assurance references the "I Am" signatures associated with Moses's radical disruption at Mount Horeb. God was with them. God came not only to calm the storm; God appeared within the storm as the disciples' deliverer. What was a moment of distress and disorientation transformed into a moment of the holy and sacred. This God was not a ghost and was very much alive. Jesus's identification on the troubled sea dispelled the disciples' fear of the unknown and gave way to awe of God's supernatural power expressed through Jesus, standing in the midst of their radical disruption.

## A CHURCH OF RADICAL DISRUPTIONS

When I first arrived at First Baptist Church of Hillside in August 2008, the membership consisted of roughly sixty active members, with a grand total of 125 listed on the church roll. The median age of this ninety-year-old American Baptist Church's congregation was fifty-four to seventy-two.

The membership consisted mostly of working- and middle-class professionals who were predominantly homeowners. The church itself is in the township of Hillside, a working-class residential municipality in Union County, New Jersey. Hillside borders the cities of Newark and Elizabeth and connects to two main thoroughfares, Route 22 and I-78. Hillside's location makes it an attractive destination for commuters who work in New York City or within the bordering counties of northern and central New Jersey. The median income for a household within the township was $59,136, and the median income for a family was $64,635.[6] Hillside is a multiethnic community of 22,456 constituents who are 34.75 percent White, 53.19 percent Black, 17.63 percent Hispanic or Latino, and 6.22 percent representing other ethnic groups within the population.[7]

Within a year's time, First Baptist Church of Hillside saw exponential growth, averaging fifteen to thirty-five new members joining every Sunday. It became customary to baptize twenty to thirty new converts at every baptism service. One traditional service at 11:00 A.M. on Sunday mornings grew into three services between Saturday evening and Sunday early afternoon. Through our targeted outreach initiatives, predominantly unchurched members of the community joined the church from as far north as North Bergen and as far south as Trenton. Many of these were young families, transient residents, and people who were either displaced or homeless. New ministries were created and new leaders developed to assist in meeting the needs of a growing church. Building modifications were made to accommodate the new growth and the increased activities happening within the life of the congregation.

Many individuals who were drawn to the church came by way of radical disruption. Some joined the church having just escaped the brutal effects of domestic violence. Others joined having fled the merciless clutching of sexual predators who ravaged their bodies without fear of violent retribution or legal consequence. There were others who joined

---

6. 2000 United States Census.
7. Ibid.

having endured a divorce that left them with nothing more than the clothes on their body. Some joined as a response to God meeting them in a moment of crisis. Then there were those who joined out of a deep desire to belong to a spiritual community or recover their familiarity with a God they knew in their childhood years. Many attested to the fact that they were content with—or otherwise ensnared by—one direction through life until God disrupted their path, much like the disciples on the Sea of Galilee, leading them in a different direction.

If the American church is to function as the incarnate hands and feet of Jesus in its communities, it must view its members as God's people who have experienced radical disruptions along their spiritual journeys. With this perspective, congregations can respond to people with compassionate acts of care, embodying the soul-calming presence of Jesus for those who are navigating sacred storms. Compassionate acts could include, for example, hosting safe spiritual retreats for battered women with children and supplying free cosmetic makeovers, assistance from hairdressers, new clothing and toys for their children, and an abundance of feminine hygiene products to safeguard their well-being. First Baptist Church of Hillside's S.I.S. Women's Ministry offers this type of support to the most vulnerable in the community regularly. The ministry also supports access to social workers, psychiatric therapists, and pastoral counselors who can help battered women work through trauma while charting a path for a new beginning. If necessary, the women can be connected to underground networks through which they escape violent abusers.

Radical acts of compassionate care can include bailing out nonviolent offenders from local prisons; providing legal representation free of charge; and extending opportunities for job-training, social networking, and financial assistance to ensure that those who have been released from prison can find adequate housing and a job. Radical forms of compassionate care can include constructing new homes for the underserved members of the local community. For instance, Cathedral International— the historic Second Baptist Church of Perth Amboy, New Jersey, under the leadership of Bishop Donald Hilliard, Jr.—constructed and sold more than a dozen townhomes in the city of Perth Amboy in response to harmful banking practices that denied applicants of color access to loans for new homes. As the congregation and its ministries grew, Cathedral International purchased a dilapidated movie theater in 1992—which at the time had become a pornographic hub for the local community—and renovated it into a spiritual center that seats fifteen hundred in its sanctuary and provides more than seventy active ministries and services to the New Jersey region.

Radical disruption needs radical compassion. Like Moses on Mount Horeb or Paul on the Damascus Road, we often find God's radical compassion in the core of a radical disruption, when God awakens our awareness to a new potential reality that transcends our own plans and desired destinations. In those moments, we encounter the presence of God, who reminds us, much like Jesus reminds the disciples on the Sea of Galilee, that we need not be afraid. The great "I Am" is with us, leading us and guiding us to different shores that confirm our purpose in the cosmic plans of God.

## LEAVING DIFFERENTLY AND DISRUPTIVELY

While waiting for the detectives from the Midtown South Precinct to allow me to leave my recording session at Unique Recording Studios, I looked out the window and gazed downward toward the street, hoping to spy any evidence of additional police presence. I could hear the howling wind straining back and forth between the skyscrapers towering over West 47th Street and 7th Avenue. Quad Studios, where Tupac had been shot, sat less than a block away on West 48th Street and 7th Avenue. The temperature was below freezing that night, and the dull city lights cast a bronze haze over Times Square. Everything felt different, but for reasons I could not adequately describe at the time.

By 1:00 P.M. on the afternoon of November 30, my entourage and I were released from Unique Recording Studios. I returned later that night to begin tracking the second version of my remix to the song, "Chill with That." I was accompanied by my friend Craig Live and production mentor D-Moet. D-Moet was a member of the rap group King Sun and D-Moet, and later produced records like Nas's single, "You Can Hate Me Now," featuring P-Diddy. By the early morning of December 1, I received another surprising visit—this time from Jive Recordings' San Francisco Bay area rapper E-40. Already a legend in Vallejo, California, E-40 was now looking for tracks to accompany his upcoming album, *In a Major Way*. While walking through the halls of Unique Recording Studios, E-40 heard an instrumental that I had co-created with producers Freak Nasty and Rodney "Darkchild" Jerkins, which I was playing in my recording room. E-40 entered my session requesting that I send him instrumentals immediately to consider for his forthcoming album.

While finishing my recording session early that morning, my two-way pager buzzed repeatedly: "911." I immediately turned on the news sitting above the console in my recording room and saw Tupac sitting in a wheelchair wearing a New York Yankees hat, a dark Nike jacket, and bandages covering the wounds from his assault. He was surrounded by paparazzi as he wheeled into the New York State Supreme Court building at 10:00 A.M. on December 1. The jurors who were considering the state's charges of sodomy and sexual assault stemming from a November 9, 1993, incident at the Parker Meridien Hotel had been sequestered; they were presumably unaware of the shooting. Tupac was acquitted of three counts of sodomy and the associated gun charges with the case but convicted of two counts of first-degree sexual abuse. After the verdict had been given, Tupac was whisked away to await sentencing on February 7, 1995.

I received several "911" messages on my pager again. This time, I was alerted that detectives from the Midtown South Precinct would be returning to do a sweep of both Quad Studios and Unique Recording Studios. It was assumed that the group present in Lil' Shawn's recording session may have discarded illegal firearms in the adjacent rooms at Quad Studios; those assumptions were transposed upon Unique Recording Studios as well. Even though I was innocent of those very assumptions, I was advised by my handlers to finish my mix immediately, grab the

DATs from the recording engineer, leave the studio, and take a different route home. So, I did—differently and disruptively.

## A LIFE OF SACRED STORMS LARGE AND SMALL

November 30 and December 1, 1994, marked my very first experiences being impacted by the orbit of the cultural phenomenon known as Tupac Amaru Shakur. The impact of those dates undergirds my point that radical disruptions can visit us in a variety of ways at different stages in our life's journey. Just as the biblical stories testify, God can visit us through naturally occurring events, tragic moments, premonitions, callings, and dreams. God not only sees us; God may disrupt our paths to ensure that God is seen by us. Sometimes these disruptions are subtle, stretching out over time. Sometimes they are cataclysmic and abrasive. Quite often, storms can send us into patterns of duress until God reveals God's self as the great "I Am" who dwells among us. Sacred storms are God's gift to us, shifting our course to help us avoid danger, choose a different career path, turn away from unhealthy relationships, confront an injustice, or bring us to a fuller understanding of our purpose and meaning in life.

How often does the church welcome in people who are disoriented from their fresh encounters with a sacred storm, and yet the church does not recognize the signs of bewilderment, the flailing oars gripped in fear. A loving church that understands the nature of life's radical disruptions can greet those feeling disrupted and unsettled with the calming presence of God. This calming presence comes through our intentionality in listening, praying, sitting, sharing, embracing, counseling, giving, and advocating. Such conscientious work of loving and serving those who struggle to make sense of life's storms and disruptions is not just reserved for the church. Leaders of corporations, governments, nonprofits, parachurch ministries, social agencies, and grassroots organizations all have a role to play in helping society dwell more peacefully, live more authentically, and find self-transcendence in the midst of life's disruptions.

Organizations like the Hip-Hop Summit Action Network, TRU Foundation, Tha Carter Fund, Keep a Child Alive, and the Dreamville Foundation have all led the way in investing in underserved communities and creating opportunities for the marginalized. When we are able to respect the presence of the divine that lives within all of us, we need not fear the uncertain or the unknown. Rather, we can take solace in knowing that, no matter our life's trajectory, we are never alone along our journey toward living life anew both in our immediate present and the future.

# 4

## GET IN

*Then he got into the boat with them and*
*the wind ceased. And they were utterly astounded,*
*for they did not understand about the loaves,*
*but their hearts were hardened.*

**—Mark 6:51–52**

W hen I first began to develop as a music producer, I benefited from the brilliant mentorship and tutelage of D-Moet. Among many other hit songs, D-Moet was the producer of the classic old school hit, "Hey Love," featuring the lyrical genius King Sun. D-Moet opened up his private recording studio in Teaneck, New Jersey, to my fledgling rap group, which went by the name Chris Large and Craig Live; I was the featured rapper and Craig Live was the singer. We were not seasoned enough to land a record deal in the early 1990s; however, we gave it our best effort, recording countless demo tapes in D-Moet's studio.

Fortunately, although my rap career never took off, my gift for music production developed rather quickly. D-Moet spent endless hours teaching me how to construct hardcore percussion patterns on the Akai MPC 60 II—a MIDI sequencer and drum sampler for many hip-hop producers in the early 1990s. (If producers weren't using the MPC 60 II to sample percussion sounds, they were most likely using the E-mu SP-1200.) D-Moet also taught me how to use the Akai S-950 to sample original music scores and implement time-stretching techniques without altering the pitch of the composition. It was because of D-Moet's teaching ability and incredible patience that I learned quickly how to compile the ingredients necessary to make a hip-hop or R&B hit. D-Moet's standard rule of thumb was, "If I turn on the radio and your song doesn't grab me within the first fifteen seconds, you don't have a hit. You have a dud presenting itself as if it were a hit."

One benefit of working out of D-Moet's studio during my early stages as a producer was meeting some of the greatest music talent in the recording industry. During the late 1980s and early to mid-1990s, Teaneck was a hotbed for famous recording artists, music composers, and producers who wanted to live outside the hustle and bustle of New York City but close enough to commute for important meetings in Midtown Manhattan. It wasn't uncommon to see songwriters and musicians from Kool & the Gang congregating in D-Moet's studio with rappers like Def Jam Recordings' artist Foxy Brown and Death Row's artist Kurupt. As early as the 1960s, groups like The Isley Brothers made the suburb of Teaneck their home and creative music incubator. One brilliant producer, songwriter, and singer who frequented D-Moet's studio was Levi Little, who hailed from Paterson, New Jersey. I took a particular liking to Levi. Along with D-Moet, Levi co-produced several of the Chris Large and Craig Live demos until he joined a new R&B group known as Blackstreet.

## ON THE ROAD TO THE SOUL TRAIN AWARDS

By July 1994, Blackstreet had taken over the airwaves as arguably the hottest R&B group in the recording industry. The group was formed by megaproducer Teddy Riley and singer Chauncey Hannibal after the abrupt dissolution of the famous R&B group Guy. Blackstreet's first record, "Baby Be Mine," was recorded for the soundtrack to Chris Rock's film *CB4*. Blackstreet followed up that soundtrack recording with hit singles like

"Booti Call" and "Before I Let You Go." Levi Little was featured as the lead singer on the third hit single, "Joy," originally written and composed for Michael Jackson. While on my way to Unique Recording Studios, traveling on a red-eye flight from California to New York, I ran into Blackstreet at the Los Angeles International Airport. The group had just arrived on a late-night flight of their own. Before traveling on private planes became a common practice, popular entertainers traveled on red-eye flights as the safest way to avoid the paparazzi. I congratulated Levi, having not seen him since we shared a recording session in D-Moet's studio two years earlier. Teddy Riley, dressed from head to toe in white, greeted me with the utmost professionalism, and Levi informed Teddy Riley that I had just produced my first record with Columbia Records' sizzling hip-hop artist Nas.

Three months later, Blackstreet was nominated by the Soul Train Music Awards for "R&B/Soul Album of the Year." They were also nominated for their hit single "Before I Let You Go." The Soul Train Music Awards would be held at the Shrine Auditorium in Los Angeles on March 13, 1995, to honor the best in R&B, soul, rap, jazz, and gospel music from the previous year. The 1995 award show was hosted by Anita Baker, Patti LaBelle, and Babyface. It included live performances from the likes of Michael Jackson, Boyz II Men, Brandy, Queen Latifah, Herbie Hancock, Warren G., along with R&B groups Gerald and Eddie Levert and Black-street. Having just been informed that my co-production with Rodney Jerkins would be featured in the soon-to-be released single "Head Nod," from the upcoming movie *Panther*, I wanted to congratulate Levi after his performance at the award show.

On March 13, five of us piled into a metallic blue Ford Taurus and headed toward the Shrine Auditorium at 665 West Jefferson Blvd to have a good time and congratulate my friend Levi for his new success as a member of Blackstreet. In the car was myself; legendary producer Spyderman, who in 1990 co-produced singles like "Poison" and "I Wanna Sex You Up" in 1991; my friend whom I consider to be closer than a brother, Brett B., a founding member of famed rap group The 7A3 and an incomparable hook connoisseur for multiplatinum rap groups like

Cypress Hill and Funkdoobiest; and two other friends of ours, all from Brooklyn. We often created music together at this townhouse in Los Angeles in between our own independent recording sessions.

As we drove south out of San Fernando Valley and toward the Los Angeles metropolitan area, I noticed a police car pulling up aggressively along the driver side of our vehicle. A white female officer proceeded to turn on a blinding white strobe light to inspect the passengers inside—a common tool for Los Angeles police officers in the 1990s, used to illuminate suspected criminals or areas deemed unsafe. After flashing the light onto the face of each person in the passenger cabin, the police officer abruptly decelerated to the rear of our Ford Taurus and proceeded to flash her siren lights.

After we pulled over near the curb, the officer did not vacate her vehicle immediately. Instead, she waited, keeping her lights flashing and the white light fixed on the rear window of our vehicle. We watched in silence as another police car pulled up behind the first. Then another squad car pulled up, followed by another. In total, five fully manned police cars pulled up with lights flashing—a showcase of excessive military force for a group of twenty-year-old musicians whom they presumed to be criminals traveling through an area in which we did not belong. Finally, the first police officer vacated her vehicle and walked toward the driver's side door. An officer from the second car left his vehicle and approached the passenger side door. While the first officer asked Spyderman for his license and registration, the other officer shined his flashlight on our faces and the floor in an up-and-down motion. After the female officer checked Spyderman's credentials, she suggested she had reason to believe that we may have been involved in a robbery. She proceeded to ask us to get out of the car and sit on the curb while she and the other officers inspected our car thoroughly.

## FLASHES OF RODNEY KING

The thought had not escaped Spyderman, Brett B., and me that this very same police department was recently captured on video committing one of the most heinous crimes in American history.[1] On March 3, 1991, Rodney Glen King was beaten by Los Angeles police officers during his arrest at the end of a nearly eight-mile pursuit for allegedly driving while intoxicated on the Interstate 210 Freeway, which runs from the Sylmar district of Los Angeles east to the Redlands. An uninvolved citizen, George Holliday, recorded Rodney King's brutal beating from his balcony and sold the video to the local news station KTLA. The raw footage showed an unarmed Rodney King on the ground being tased and mercilessly beaten by four officers. Rodney was struck fifty-six times by the batons of the officers on the scene, suffering a fractured leg, multiple face fractures, and numerous bruises and contusions covering his entire body. The incident captured on video was subsequently sold by KTLA to CNN, who then shared their broadcast with news media around the world. Upon King's release from LAPD custody, after the charge of "felony evading" was dropped against him, the world was able to witness his injuries: a broken right leg in a cast, his face badly cut and swollen, bruises covering his body, and a burn area on his chest from the jolt of a stun gun. The violence of the LAPD caused a public furor.

At a press conference, Los Angeles police chief Daryl Gates announced to the community that four of the officers involved, Sergeant Stacey Koon, Lawrence Powell, Timothy Wind, and Ted Briseno would be disciplined for their use of excessive force. On March 15, Sergeant Koon and officers Powell, Wind, and Briseno were indicted by a Los Angeles grand jury. All four were officially charged with assault with a deadly weapon and excessive use of force by a police officer. Koon, as the commanding officer on the scene, was charged with aiding and abetting the beating. Powell and Koon were also charged with falsifying their reports. Of the four officers who were eventually tried on charges of use of excessive force, three were acquitted. The twelve-person jury issued

---

1. This landscape became the breeding ground for the rap group N.W.A., whose controversial first album *Straight Outta Compton* explicitly depicted their experience with police brutality in southern Los Angeles.

three verdicts of not guilty and failed to reach a verdict on one charge for the fourth, Officer Powell. Within hours of the acquittals, the 1992 Los Angeles riots started, sparked by outrage among racial minorities over the trial's verdict and related, longstanding social issues. In six days of violence, beginning on April 29, 1992, more than sixty people were killed, more than two thousand were injured, and nearly $1 billion in property was destroyed. On May 1, President George H. W. Bush ordered military troops and riot-trained federal officers to control the unrest. Under heavy pressure from the Los Angeles political establishment, Rodney King advocated for a peaceful end to the conflict.

On April 17, 1993, the federal government successfully prosecuted a civil rights case, convicting Sergeant Koon and Officer Powell for violations of King's civil rights; the other two officers were acquitted. Koon and Powell were sentenced to two-and-a-half years in prison for the cruel and cynical beating of Rodney King. In a separate civil lawsuit in 1994, a jury found the City of Los Angeles liable and awarded King $3.8 million in damages. The LAPD did not take these convictions or King's monetary award lightly. In speaking with other artists and music producers who visited Los Angeles during 1994 and 1995, it felt as though the LAPD increased their strategic targeting and racial profiling of hip-hop entertainers immediately following the prosecution of Sergeant Koon and Officer Powell.

Minority communities in Los Angeles were well acquainted with the LAPD's use of blunt force to contain growing Black and Brown populations. Aggressive dispersion tactics—such as the use of police dogs, fire hoses, and skull-cracking police batons—echoed the suffering endured by Black communities in Los Angeles as far back as the Watts riots of 1965. On August 11, 1965, a twenty-one-year-old African American male named Marquette Frye was pulled over in Watts, Los Angeles, for drunk driving. After failing a field sobriety test, police officers attempted to place Marquette under arrest. The police alleged that Marquette resisted arrest, prompting a confrontation between Marquette, the arresting officers, and Marquette's mother, Rena Frye, during which the police violently bludgeoned Marquette over the head with a baton. A crowd of onlookers shouted their dismay at the violence against Marquette. Rumors began to spread that the squadrons of backup police who arrived on the scene began to beat the innocent bystanders mercilessly, and that one officer kicked a pregnant woman who stood in protest. For six days, riots broke out all over the city in protest against racism and a violent police department that had held Watts under siege for far too long.

Nearly fourteen thousand members of the California Army National Guard were brought in to suppress the protests by force, which led to at least thirty-four deaths and nearly $40 million in property damage. Underlying the Watts protests was a growing frustration within a Black community that had migrated from the South to seek employment and freedom from Jim Crow laws. These Black migrants arrived in cities like Detroit, Chicago, St. Louis, Philadelphia, and Los Angeles as early as 1915—the beginning of the Great Migration—to pursue jobs in newly established manufacturing industries within northern and western US cities. Rather than accommodate these newcomers, city officials passed laws to exclude migrants from equal access to jobs and schools. Rather than reform long-standing, racially restrictive housing "covenants," city elites militarized their police departments to restrain and terrorize Black and Brown communities.

In 1950, William H. Parker was appointed and sworn in as the new Los Angeles chief of police. After the scandal of Bloody Christmas of 1951, when members of the police department savagely beat five Mexican Americans and two white Americans, Chief Parker advocated for an independent police department free from the political pressures that he argued would hinder the creation of a more professionalized police force in the city. The general public supported Chief Parker's proposal, granting a charter that effectively isolated the Los Angeles Police Department from the oversight of city government. By 1960, the LAPD was promoted as one of the best police departments in the world—despite the criticism Chief Parker received from leaders in the city's Black and Brown communities prior to the Watts riots of 1965.

As Spyderman, Brett B., and I sat on the edge of the curb, all I could think of was a common scene from a plethora of Black exploitation films made in the 1970s in which the white male officer plants a gun to substantiate false claims made against a person of color. With great anxiety, I watched each officer as they pried open the trunk, looked between the seats, searched the glove compartment, tapped the tires, and rummaged through the floorboards. My colleagues and I were all keenly aware of the other officers standing outside of their respective patrol cars with one hand resting upon their firearm, almost expecting a gun to turn up in the search. The most disturbing part of this illegal interrogation was the number of cars that passed by slowly as they gazed upon what they perceived to be the scene of a crime. With each passing car we watched individuals nodding their heads in disgust. Some wagged their fingers with righteous indignation. Others rolled down their windows, shouting, "Get out of our neighborhood" or "Go find another place to get high!"

Neither the police officers nor the passersby could ever imagine that three of us on that curb were responsible for having generated over a quarter of a billion dollars in record sales over the last two years. It had not dawned on—or was irrelevant to—the officers and passersby alike that their own inhumane actions framed us as guilty-until-proven-innocent rather than innocent-until-proven-guilty. No one intervened to see if we needed any assistance. Not one pedestrian considered the thought that we were very young adults forced to sit curbside, in a vulnerable position, thousands of miles away from home, without any legal representation. It did not cross the minds of those driving by that we were being racially profiled. They watched, but they refused to get involved. The first officer assumed that there had to be something suspicious about five young Black males traveling in a car together in that ZIP code. The culture at the time suggested that nothing good could come from a car filled with young Black men.

## ON THE ROAD FROM JERUSALEM TO JERICHO

With the disturbing memory of Rodney King's brutal assault lingering in our minds, Spyderman, Brett B., and I sat silently, waiting for an unjustified aggression to be sent in our direction for simply being too young and too Black in an all-white neighborhood. It would be hard for a well-read Bible student not to recognize certain parallels between our foreboding situation on the side of Figueroa Drive and the parable of the Good Samaritan (Luke 10:30–37). The Gospel of Luke frames the parable with the question raised by a religious scholar for Jesus to answer: "What must I do to inherit eternal life?" (Luke 10:25). This scholar, a lawyer with impeccable academic credentials, studied God's law and played a critical role in interpreting the law so the Jews of his day would know how to obey it. In addition, the scholar played a pivotal role in helping to administer justice within the Jewish system. People respected his expertise. On this particular day, the expert of the law had a question he desired to share with Jesus—and not simply share with Jesus, but use as a test of Jesus's teaching. If Jesus responded with the wrong answer, his error would surely diminish his following and lead the gathered audience back to the Pharisees and the teachers of the law—the more qualified religious leaders in the community.

For his question, the religious scholar raised a topic that was commonly debated among the rabbis of that time: Since God had given the people of Israel an inheritance (namely the land of Israel) that the people had then forfeited through disobedience, what now was the holy inheritance? The religious scholar gave Jesus an opportunity to provide a new definition when he asked, "What must I do to inherit eternal life?"

In rhetorical fashion, Jesus bounced the question back to the religious scholar: "What is written in the law?" (Luke 10:26). Both knew the law had to be interpreted for modern times, so Jesus asked for the lawyer's own interpretation. Now the lawyer was being tested, not Jesus.

True to his profession, the scholar quoted the scriptures (Deuteronomy 6:4–5 and Leviticus 19:18)—ironically aligning himself with Jesus rather than causing the intended theological wedge. Love your God and love your neighbor, wholeheartedly. Then you will be and do what God expects.

Not satisfied with the outcome of his first question, the religious scholar tried again: "Who is my neighbor?" (Luke 10:29). In other words, how far should an observer of God's law extend? Jewish legal interpretation of God's law sought clear definition for every person and relationship: Jew and Gentile, Jew and Roman, man and woman, free man and slave, priest and laity, clean and unclean, righteous and sinner, alike. Those definitions determined how and when a person could participate in Jewish worship.

Jesus responded with a parabolic answer, a rhetorical form he often used to teach on the mysteries God's realm. He used a scene that was familiar to his listening audience: the seventeen-mile road from Jerusalem down to Jericho, which extended through a mountain pass and fell almost thirty-three hundred feet in elevation. This road was well-traveled by both the poor and the aristocrats. It was known, ominously, as the "Way of Blood." Government officials, Jewish leaders, religious pilgrims, and many others frequently made the trip on the "Way of Blood" from Jerusalem to Jericho.[2] Criminals took advantage of the elites' need to travel this winding, crooked road through dangerous passes. They often hid behind the large rocks above the narrow passes and preyed on travelers.

In Jesus's parable, a traveler using the "Way of the Blood" was attacked, stripped of his clothing, beaten mercilessly, and left for dead on the side of the road. Jesus then told of passersby who witnessed the traveler's desperate situation: A priest, the highest of Jewish religious leaders, hurriedly stepped to the other side of the road and continued on his important business, even though rabbinic law expected him to bury any corpse he discovered. Similarly, a Levite, who carried out the more mundane tasks of temple worship and operation, passed quickly by. As Jesus shared his parable, the crowd waited for a helper to appear in the story and aid the beaten traveler; the elite and respected leaders of the parable disappointed them. Instead, Jesus gave his audience a Samaritan, a traveler who in Jewish eyes had little reason to be in Jewish territory and who would be the last person to qualify as a loving neighbor. Samaritans and Jews historically despised each other. However, Jesus

---

2. I. Howard Marshall, *The Gospel of Luke: A Commentary on the Greek Text* (Grand Rapids, MI: Paternoster Press, William B. Eerdmans, 1978), 444.

used his rhetorical genius to show the Samaritan's actions as the full embodiment of what Jesus defined as neighborly love, using the religious scholar's own interpretation of law.

From the dying man's perspective in the ditch, anyone who offered first aid and emergency assistance was a true loving neighbor. For Jesus, the Samaritan had *compassion*—a Greek expression built on the word for a person's deep inner parts, the seat of emotions and feelings. *Compassion* encapsulated Jesus's feeling for those in need (for examples, see Matthew 9:36, 14:14, 15:32, 20:34; Mark 1:41, 6:34, 8:2; Luke 7:13). This was true neighborly love—a love beyond anything civic or religious law expects, a love that acts simply because of the extreme need of another. The Samaritan was the one loving enough to take the dying man from the ditch and restore him to life under supervised care, without cost to the suffering man (Luke 10:35). In the parable, the Samaritan was not merely someone who should be loved as a neighbor. The Samaritan became the hero of the story, the person showing love, the one whose love others should imitate. Jesus told the religious scholar—and the listening audience—to go and show mercy like the Samaritan had done.

## JESUS DOESN'T MIND GETTING IN

In parables and actions, Jesus modeled what it meant to serve selflessly and to respect the humanity of others. When the disciples panicked on their boat under stormy circumstances they could neither control nor handle, Jesus took action to relieve their crisis. He did not judge them for their failure to realize that he commanded the waters and the winds. Like a Samaritan who did not wait for a Jewish traveler to repent of personal bias before offering aid, Jesus did not wait for the disciples to learn their lesson before he stepped into their storm.

Jesus made the courageous decision to walk on the water and meet the disciples where they were—instinctively knowing how deflated the disciples had become. It takes courage to walk in the direction most would walk away from, especially with willful intention. Leading into the wind means moving toward the societal issues and systemic structures hindering progress, being undeterred by the inherited biases and hidden assumptions that constrain justice. Without courage, one cannot lead into the wind to uplift those who struggle at the oar in the middle of a storm.

Leading into the wind is one thing. Making the decision to get into the boat is another. Mark 6:51 begins, "Then he got into the boat with them . . ." suggesting that Jesus saw value in meeting the disciples where they were, rather than insisting that the disciples meet Jesus where he was going (Mark 6:51). Ordinarily, when a person or team of individuals set out for sail, they create a rope ladder and tie it to one side of the boat so that it was available to any individuals who fell out of the vessel. Rope ladders were always reachable. If a sea-faring individual didn't have a rope ladder, it was customary to tie a rope in a U-shape on any side of the boat for the same purpose. Anyone who fell overboard could use this rope to gain support by placing their leg in the rope and using their leg strength as leverage to get back into the boat. Mark's Gospel makes no mention of a ladder or a U-shaped rope. Quite likely, the disciples were so engulfed in the unpredictable storm that they either forgot to offer Jesus a way to get onboard or they had no such device at their disposal. As with other supernatural experiences concerning Jesus, including the most recent feeding of the five thousand (Mark 6:30–44), fear and amazement paralyzed the faith of the disciples. Even though they interacted with Jesus daily, they failed to understand his person and mission. They were unable to recognize Jesus as the divine commander of their storms, or to believe Jesus was more than a ghost that might float his way onto their boat. Either way, Jesus "got in," undeterred by the distress of the disciples on the Sea of Galilee.

I wish, when I first gave my life to Jesus Christ, that I could say the church-at-large "got into" my boat, which at the time felt like it was capsizing. Unfortunately, I did not experience Jesus through my interactions with the church in that way. To be frank, had Jesus not radically disrupted my life in the way that he did, I probably would not have remained with the church. The visions of my initial conversion experience and subsequent discipleship journey still remain fresh in my mind:

I remember wearing the leather motorcycle jacket, Timberland boots, Karl Kani jeans with one pant leg rolled up to my knee, the silk white BVD t-shirt, the gold rope chain, and the diamond earring in my left ear at the altar when I first gave my life to Christ. I also remember the black Lexus coup and the egg-white Toyota 4-Runner. I remember living in homes on both coasts. I remember the S-curl and the gold caps I would wear on my teeth for special occasions. These were all markers of a hip-hop culture that embraced me fully. This is the person I had become when Jesus first appeared with the question: "Will you follow me?"

Yet I remember it being impressed upon me that my public presentation would not "fit" the expectations of the Black middle-class church. I remember the idea being conveyed that I should strive for a more refined presentation and shun the hip-hop identity that had become my own—especially if I intended to respond to God's call to preach. These suggestions, both spoken and unspoken, caused a spiritual dilemma for me. Rather than experiencing Jesus as one who "got in" with me, unfortunately, I experienced a Jesus who insisted that I "get in" with him and then walk alone through the stormy waters of my own spiritual transformation. The Jesus I experienced in my studio, the one who "got in" with me at the tail end of my mixing session for Janet Jackson, was quite different from the Jesus presented in many Black middle-class churches.

## THE CHURCH HAS TO GET IN TOO

For the reasons just mentioned, I have always made it my ambition to "get in" with people rather than insist that they "get in" with me. I believe Mark 6:51 is an example that Jesus teaches the church, offering a compass by which we can both detect the SOS signal coming from those struggling at the oars of life and be compelled to "get in" with them to help calm the raging winds that have assailed their hopes, dreams, and life ambitions. To "get in" is to accept the young praise team leader who may not have anything more than a club outfit to wear to church. To "get in" is to accept the single mother who may have to work three jobs to support her child through college. To "get in" is to accept the couple who are not married but have made an economic decision to cohabitate as a means to keep their heads above water. To "get in" is to love the young person who identifies as LGBTQIA and loves God just as much as the cisgendered and heterosexual within the church. To "get in" is to celebrate and affirm our women clergy as much as we do our male clergy.

To "get in" also means stepping into the local community—not waiting for the community to "get it" with our church—in order to advocate on behalf of the marginalized and the poor. It means providing shelter for the homeless and substance for the under- and unemployed. It means offering after-school tutoring, job training, financial literacy programs, reentry initiatives, and developmental life skill modules for youth to become, at the bare minimum, gainfully employed, if not successful entrepreneurs in their industry of choice. It means offering second language courses for those segments of the population who speak English as a second or third language. It means advocating on behalf of children who will be pulled through subpar public school systems, encouraged to secure loans for a college many will be ill-equipped to attend, and then kicked to the curb if they are not able to meet the academic standards at the college of their choosing.

Until recently, the Black church has always taken the lead in "getting in" with the downtrodden and the systemically oppressed. Getting in is what has made the Black church so distinct as a spiritual institution of hope for those who have suffered under the tyranny of slavery, lynching, overt racism, and exclusion since America's inception. Leaders like A.M.E. Bishop Daniel A. Payne, Bishop Richard Allen, and Bishop Henry McNeal Turner dedicated their lives to fighting against government-sanctioned mob violence, which claimed the lives of so many Black and Brown bodies before and after the Civil War. They devoted themselves to building a new Christian community for former African slaves who had been forced to stand in balconies during worship in white-only churches, while also founding colleges, designing clergy training programs to enhance the literacy of their churches, providing economic relief for those who migrated from plantations in the South, and building social institutions to service the needs of growing Black communities in the North. Leaders like Rev. Alexander Crummell cultivated a new Pan-Africanist cultural hermeneutic to help Black constituents reimagine what it meant to be fully human and wholly loved by God. Servant leaders and powerful proclaimers like Miss Betsey Stockton, Rev. Theodore S. Wright, Rev. Jarena Lee, Rev. John Gloucester, Rev. Francis James Grimké, and Rev. Dr. Charles Allen Stillman embodied a living word that crashed through social ceilings and kicked down ideological doors hindering the progress of a people who were determined to keep rising as a liberated people of God.

For decades, the Black church had no choice but to "get in" with the oppressed and underserved to protect the dignity of its constituency, which suffered under micro and macro attacks of white supremacy. Today, the church must "get in" on conversations concerning why it is no longer viewed as a central pillar of community health. Anecdotal and statistical evidence suggests that Gen X, Millennials, and Gen Z now look to other spiritual practices and alternative communities to find support and a sense of belonging. They congregate in virtual spaces, coffee shops, wellness centers, nontraditional Sunday brunch spots, and other public spaces. Members of the younger generations who do come to church prefer nonconventional worship gatherings and often bring an entirely different set of postpandemic social needs. In addition, patterns of age and race, gentrification, rising real estate costs, and unstable housing trends have made the historical Black church more susceptible to closing than ever before. The church, and especially the Black church, can ill-afford to insist its younger neighbors "get in" with the congregation without first figuring out how to "get in" with where the people are today.

Getting in will require a total reimagining of what it means to be a church—and a church member—in this postquarantine era. Leaders will need to rethink the social context in which theology is curated before they can find a new divinely inspired language that reaches the hearts of today's generations. If younger generations prefer community spaces traditionally considered to be secular, the church will need to "get in" those spaces and do so with the love and concern Jesus shared with the disciples trapped at sea. It will be nearly impossible for the church to remain a collaborating partner in social equity, purpose, and meaning if the church refuses to meet people in the middle of their sacred storms. To "get in" is to engage in more creatively constructed experiences that allow the church to meet the people where they are as they are. Getting in should lead to more imaginative ways of affirming our humanity, rather than sticking to the same religious traditions that have caused more harm than good. For instance, Dr. Leslie D. Callahan, senior pastor of the St. Paul's Baptist Church in Philadelphia, led an open discussion on Facebook questioning the ill-informed assumptions churches make regarding how people experience the typical Mother's Day worship service. To Dr. Callahan's point, one cannot assume that all Christians have healthy relationships with their mothers. Therefore, the church must choose a more compassionate, authentic, and creative way to acknowledge those individuals who feel triggered by the traditional Mother's Day worship service. I agree with Dr. Callahan. Getting in should lead to peace and inclusiveness. The fruit of getting in should be the forming of newly resurrected communities without causing harm to those who do not agree with or enjoy some of the church's traditional religious practices.

Finally, if we are to "get in" as Jesus did, we will be required to rethink what it means to be human and whole—no matter one's ethnicity, class, gender, or sexual orientation. If we are true followers of Jesus, we will need to "get in" with the pursuit of peace, happiness, and justice for all of God's children. We need prophetic preaching and the teaching from the likes of Bishop Yvette Flunder, senior pastor and founder of the City of Refuge Church of Christ in Oakland, California, to help us find our way—or, more importantly, to help us find God's way as it relates to loving our neighbor in the way God loves us.[3] Mark's Gospel reminds us that Jesus, after seeing his disciples' struggle, took the only step one who loves God and neighbor could possibly take: Jesus got in with the disciples to calm the storm and to calm their hearts. If we claim to be his disciples,

---

3. McMickle, *Where Have All the Prophets Gone?*

we will "get in" with the underserved, marginalized, and misunderstood no matter where they are. If our driving motive for being—as Christians and as the church—is our unwavering love for God, we will walk on water, if need be, to remind others that God is with them. Not only is God with them, God intends to dwell among them as they journey toward safe ground. Today's youth and young adults have witnessed far too many Christians sidestep the wounded traveler who is simply looking for love. Today's women clergy, members of the LGBTQIA community, our children, elderly, and the othered among us are tired of a church that turns away while life's storms threaten to rob them of their full humanity. The church needs to "get in" to remind those who struggle at the oar that this too shall pass.

## THE AFTERMATH

After we sat on the curb for almost an hour, the interrogating officers informed us that we could stand, and they returned our personal identifications. It was explained to us that they had received an anonymous call from someone suggesting we looked like we were on our way to rob a bank in the area. Someone thought that five young Black men driving in a car in that section of the community seemed suspicious. The obvious reason we were apprehended was because we had been "othered." Despite the fact that we were all draped with diamond encrusted gold chains and platinum jewelry worthy of a coronation ceremony, our skin tone, hip-hop swag, and freedom of movement posed a threat to a community that was accustomed to excluding Black youth and young adults from its confined borders. This community felt threatened by the presence of a group of young Black men who were simply passing by. The police officers on the scene happily complied with the cultural norms of that community, reinforcing that we were not welcome "there."

We piled back into the Ford Taurus, quietly. Over a quarter of a billion dollars worth of young musical talent had been silenced under the script of "probable cause." As we traveled further south on Figueroa Street, we saw the Moroccan-styled architecture of the Shrine Auditorium in the distance. Upon entering the VIP section in the parking lot, I saw rapper Treach from the hip-hop trio Naughty by Nature standing at the top of the staircase, draped in Walker Wear and what looked like a five-pound silver dog chain hanging around his neck. R&B singer Brandi stood not too far away in what appeared to be a light jean top with black silk dress pants. Mary J. Blige walked into the front entrance with her entourage. Patti LaBelle was chatting with Boyz II Men just to our right. Death Row recording artist Snoop Dogg and CEO Suge Knight were talking with Aaliyah and her management team. So So Def's Da Brat was standing with CEO and megaproducer Jermaine Dupri. Debbie Allen was not too far off in the distance making small talk with Def Jam Recordings' Warren G. The R&B group Brownstone was engaged in a jovial conversation with Queen Latifah.

The buzz in the parking lot was that Michael Jackson (who, several years later, featured my recorded performance of Biggie on his single "Unbreakable") would be performing live to commemorate the twenty-fifth anniversary of the Soul Train Music Awards. Record company executives, media representatives, and unsigned artists all pressed their way through the crowd, intermingling as they gravitated toward the inner sanctuary to view the show. Light bulbs flashed in the hands of the paparazzi. Pimps stood across the street pushing sex workers forward to entice the artists making their way into the interior court of the Shrine. Drug dealers walked through the crowd, hoping to sell their carefully prepared street pharmaceuticals. I never got the opportunity to reconnect with my friend Levi from Blackstreet; I was too numb to engage in meaningful conversation with anyone. As Spyderman, Brett B., and I attended numerous record company after-parties later that evening, all I could think of was being accosted like the traveler making his way south to Jericho. Images of paddy rollers monitoring and enforcing violent discipline upon slaves in the Antebellum South flooded my mind. I thought of how many passersby gazed upon us as we sat, disruptively apprehended, just outside of Panorama City. No one had the courage to "get in." None saw the need to enter the chaos with us to help navigate our unexpected storm.

# 5

## CARING STRATEGIES FOR LANDING DIFFERENTLY

*When they had crossed over, they came to land
at Gennesaret and moored the boat.*

**—Mark 6:53**

For those of us who lived in the Bedford-Stuyvesant section of Brooklyn, New York, during the 1980s and early 1990s and were not raised in the church, we were unaware of our proximity to prophetic voices like Dr. Gardner C. Taylor at Concord Baptist Church of Christ, Dr. William Augustus Jones Jr. at Bethany Baptist Church, Dr. Sandy F. Ray at Cornerstone Baptist Church, Bishop Marvin D. Williams at Greater St. Stephen United Church of God, Rev. Clarence Norman at First Baptist Church of Crown Heights, and Dr. Johnny Youngblood at St. Paul Baptist Church. In the summer of 1988, our pastors were Eric B. & Rakim, Run-DMC, Big Daddy Kane, KRS-One, Biz Markie, MC Lyte, and Public Enemy. Our deacons were the Ultramagnetic MCs, LL Cool J, Audio Two, Stetsasonic, Kool G Rap, and EPMD. Our on-call ministers were N.W.A., Super Lover Cee & Casanova Rud, Doug E. Fresh, and DJ Jazzy Jeff & the Fresh Prince. When the unchurched youth of Brooklyn were looking for solace and a sense of meaning in life, we turned to the voices of Slick Rick, Heavy D, Dana Dane, and Whodini.

Whodini's singles like "One Love," "Big Mouth," "Funky Beat," "You Brought It on Yourself," and "Escape (I Need a Break)" counseled us as we attempted to make sense of our jagged urban landscape. In between the broken crack vials, heroin needles, and bullet casings that littered our local parks were the footprints of a youth movement that turned to hip-hop as a cultural art form to channel our hopes, dreams, and unbridled anger against the systems of oppression stifling our social progress. By 1991, Whodini began to lose steam in an industry beginning to pivot away from conscious rap and toward a new genre of hip-hop labeled "gangster rap." A plethora of new artists and rap groups like Geto Boys, N.W.A., Scarface, and Compton's Most Wanted ascended to the top of the charts. Songs like "A Minute to Pray and a Second to Die," "Original Gangster," and "Steady Mobbin'" took centerstage. Whodini's two singles "Judy/Inside the Joint" and "Smilin' Faces Sometimes" landed at #73 and #65 on the US R&B charts—a far cry from #4 in 1984 when Whodini released the popular "Friends/Five Minutes of Funk."

By 1996, record companies put their full commitment and investment capital toward gangster rap. New artists like Jay-Z, The Notorious B.I.G., Mobb Deep, Nas, 2Pac, M.O.P., Snoop Dogg, Foxy Brown, Ghostface Killah, Method Man, WC, Mack 10, Ice Cube, and Redman competed against the likes of Bone Thugs-N-Harmony, OutKast, Coolio, Busta Rhymes, Lost Boyz, the Roots, and the Fugees for top rating on the hip-hop and R&B charts. The rise of hip-hop was solidified, following the release of the most important album to hit the American charts in 1991: N.W.A.'s *Niggaz4life*, which supplanted rock band R.E.M.'s album *Out of Time* as the top-selling album. Corporate executives in the music industry could no longer deny the legitimacy of hip-hop as a cultural art form and, more importantly, of gangster rap's appeal to youth both in the inner city and middle America.

The oppression of the Black body could be felt in songs like "Straight Outta Compton" and "Fuck Tha Police." The perpetual rage of Black and

Brown youth in urban centers across the country was expressed in songs like Cypress Hill's "How I Could Just Kill a Man" as a response to the death-dealing social policies introduced through Reaganomics. Poverty rose to the rate of 31.6 percent for all black Americans. Lingering attitudes from the Reagan administration pinned the rise of Black crime on the broken Black family rather than the result of vicious cutbacks of social services that were critical to the livelihood of the working-class family in the inner city. Political conservatives stigmatized violent crime in Black communities as a symptom of an inherent flaw within the entire Black race. Homicide became the leading cause of death for Black males aged fifteen to twenty-five. Corporate record executives made the conscious decision to profit off of gangster rap at the expense of the Black death. By the end of 1991, pioneering rap groups like Whodini were thoroughly overtaken by a new sound, which gave voice to the downtrodden and the oppressed in ghettos across the nation.

## MY MELLO MY MAN

In between recording and mixing the record I produced that featured Shaq and Biggie, I was invited into a music project aimed to bring Whodini back to prominence in the music industry. The famous Brooklyn-based trio consisted of John "Ecstasy" Fletcher, Jalil Hutchins, and their world-renowned turntable artist DJ Drew, commonly known as "Grandmaster Dee." Whodini was one of the very first rap groups in the early 1980s to intertwine R&B music with rap, laying the foundation for a new genre of music: "New Jack Swing." The group broke into the recording industry in 1982 with their first single, "Magic's Wand," which combined the synthetic sounds of disco music with electro-rap; it was the very first hip-hop record accompanied by a music video. Whodini also had the distinction of being the first rap group to include break-dancers in their live performances. One of the very first dancers to tour and perform with Whodini was a talented twelve-year-old named Jermaine Dupri.

Jermaine Dupri eventually established his own record label, So So Def, in 1993. Not too soon after receiving his label imprint under the banner of Columbia Records, Dupri discovered the female R&B group Xscape. That same year, he met and signed female rapper Da Brat to his record label, an introduction facilitated by the rap duo Kris Kross that Dupri discovered in 1991. By 1995, Dupri collaborated with platinum artist Mariah Carey on her hit single "Always Be My Baby"; he produced and co-wrote singles for MC Lyte, Usher, and the Braxtons. As a sign of respect to the rap group who gave him his start in the record business, Dupri agreed to sign Whodini to a record deal. This new opportunity allowed Whodini to reestablish a career path that had been disrupted by the onset and commercialization of gangster rap. Every producer who agreed to work on this project—including me—was bestowed the privilege of joining Jermaine Dupri in cultivating a new sound for this illustrious rap group and their reemergence in a transforming industry. At the time of Whodini's signing, members of the group were working as EMTs and sound technicians. It was our goal to change that.

The creative process with Whodini began with the tracking of the music at Chung King Studios, located in the Hudson Square neighborhood of New York City. By 1996, Chung King Studios became my favorite place to create musically. Albums like *Radio* by LL Cool J, *Raising Hell* by Run-DMC, *Licensed to Ill* by the Beastie Boys, and *It Takes a Nation of Millions to Hold Us Back* by Public Enemy were all produced in this hallowed space. As I laid the selected music onto two-inch reels, legendary Bronx rapper Fat Joe walked into the room with members of the rugged production team the Beatnuts. Fat Joe was at the studios to present music and a creative concept to those spearheading Shaq's soon-to-be-released album. A member of the famous production team Trackmasters, Dave Atkinson, also entered my session. At the time, Dave co-produced the popular single "Affirmative Action" for Nas's record *It Was Written*. My father and a group of other acquaintances also present had just ordered lobster, garlic shrimp, and ginger ale from the per diem I had been given to cover the cost of meals while in the studio.

For the development of the lyrical creative concept, I once again turned to my dear friend Clean Cut. Clean Cut was famously known as the guest rapper on a myriad of R&B singles, including Christopher Williams's "I'm Dreaming" and Keith Sweat's "Keep It Coming." Just the year before, I produced a record featuring Clean Cut on an Immortal Records compilation entitled *The Next Chapter*. The name of Clean Cut's single was "For All My Peoples."

As we bobbed our heads to the syncopation of the drum kick, hard snare, and xylophone chords projecting over the studio monitors, Clean Cut tapped my shoulder. "I got it," he said. "I have the perfect hook to bring the best out of Whodini. I want to call this song 'My Mello My Man.'"

Clean Cut's idea was brilliant. Borrowing from rap metaphors used as far back as 1980 by the rap groups Family Four and Crash Crew, Clean Cut spit the perfect hook in tempo with the track: "Jahlil . . . ah my mello my man . . . Ecstasy . . . ah my mello my man . . . Grandmaster Dee . . . ah my mello my man . . . Who-di-ni . . . rock the house!" At least for a moment, in the blue room of Chung King Studios, it felt as though Whodini had the chance to land successfully in the new hip-hop ecosystem. We all chanted the hook repeatedly. A new beginning was at hand. Different, but very new.[1]

## THE LANDING PLACE OF THE DISRUPTED

Mark's Gospel (6:45) states rather pointedly that when the disciples initially set out from the place where Jesus fed the five thousand, Jesus instructed them to travel across the Sea of Galilee to a village named Bethsaida. While crossing the sea to Bethsaida, the disciples were stopped on their journey by the velocity of unexpected winds. The storm's force was so severe the

---

1. Unfortunately, this song would not be included in the final version of Whodini's album *Six* that was released in late 1996. It was suggested that "My Mello My Man" did not fit the creative direction Jermaine Dupri envisioned for the album. However, Whodini performed this song at many of their live showcases in the fall and winter of 1996. It is quite common for a song to not make the final cut of an album but still be included in a rotation developed for live performances. In some instances, a song that may have been excluded from an album may receive more attention and promotion than the songs that made the cut. Unreleased hip-hop classics like Kanye West's "All Day" featuring Kendrick Lamar, Young Nudy and Pi'erre Bourne's "Pissy Pamper" featuring Playboi Carti, and Lil Wayne's "Scottie Pippen" are examples.

disciples were completely blown off course. Instead of Bethsaida, the disciples landed in a heavily populated place called Gennesaret (also called the Plain of Gennesaret), a region that curved along the northwestern section of Sea of Galilee. This region was known to have fertile soil complemented with flowing streams and rivers. First-century historian Flavius Josephus referred to Gennesaret as the most preferable site for agricultural development during the first century.[2] Rabbis coined the region "the Garden of God." The fruits of Gennesaret were so exceptional that the rabbis did not allow them in Jerusalem during feast observances, fearing many would attend only to enjoy their succulence. In addition to well-developed waterways, the land was covered with trees; walnut, palm, olive, and fig groves flourished in the temperate area. Harvests of grapes, rice, wheat, vegetables, melons, and wildflowers were abundant. The distinct richness of the area was an attraction not only to the Israelites but to the Roman officials, political elites, and wealthy merchants. Countless shipping boats adorned the shores of Gennesaret, and the frequency of unexpected storms on the sea drew residents and travelers alike to the shoreline where they could watch nature's drama unfold.

The region was also a place through which the sick, poor, powerless, and displaced traveled, en route to the city of Tiberias. Tiberias sat lakeside just south of Gennesaret; it was the destination for disgruntled citizens with a case to plead before Herod Antipas, the tetrarch and Roman vassal. They came by boat, chariot, wagon, or on foot, and the well-traveled paths to and through Gennesaret made the region a hub of knowledge. Scores of travelers came to the area having either heard about Jesus's supernatural healing power or having experienced his wonder-working healing power themselves. Thus when the disciples moored their boat in Gennesaret and Jesus stepped onto the shore, people immediately recognized him. No matter their social location, the people gathered en masse to receive a touch from Jesus. More importantly, the disciples again bore witness to

---

2. Henry Baker Tristam, *The Physical Geography, Geology, and Meteorology of the Holy Land* (Piscataway, NJ: Gorgias Press, 2007).

the steadfast trajectory of Jesus's purpose and mission, regardless of the unexpected storm that blew them off course. With this reminder, one could even conclude that the unexpected storm drew the disciples closer to God's purpose and mission, rather further away from it.

## CARING STRATEGIES FOR LANDING DIFFERENTLY

But before they landed in Gennesaret, after Jesus had calmed the storm and joined the disciples on their boat, the Gospel of Mark does not tell us what Jesus said to the disciples. What were those conversations like? Did the disciples question why their path had been altered or whether they would reroute to Bethsaida? Did Jesus know in advance that the disciples' path would change? When did the disciples realize that Gennesaret was their new destination? Did the disciples question whether they were equipped to handle the new demands in Gennesaret once they landed? What about their feelings of inadequacy during and after the storm? These were fishermen, after all; they should have been well adjusted to the unexpected demands common to traveling at sea. Did they feel as though they failed Jesus's expectations in the same way they did during the feeding of the five thousand? Maybe they felt as though following Jesus's instruction when life got hard was too hard of a task. What was Jesus's pastoral approach or clinical method, if any, to bolster the disciples' faith and their belonging within his mission, after first reassuring them, according to Mark 6:50, "Take heart, it is I; do not be afraid"? Mark doesn't tell us what Jesus said in the boat, but we know that Jesus sat in it with the disciples. He landed with them at the new, unexpected destination.

Dr. Taft Quincey Heatley notes in his text *The Pandemic Pastor: Leadership Wisdom for Ministry During Difficult Times* that the COVID-19 pandemic disrupted norms for the entire world—from the availability of essential supplies to the typical ways of doing business.[3] What the

---

3. Taft Quincey Heatley, *The Pandemic Pastor: Leadership Wisdom for Ministry During Difficult Times* (Heritage Publishing, 2022).

world once took for granted had become dislodged by a necessity to adapt to a new reality. The pandemic challenged the practices of corporations and civic organizations, exposing the inequities inherent in our global support systems for all to see. Similarly, the church and all of its systems, structures, traditions, and beliefs were called into question due to the impact of the pandemic. Pastors and church leaders were reintroduced to the limits, weaknesses, and flaws of their local church. Congregations that failed to launch a virtual presence before the pandemic suffered an abrupt disconnect from their members during the initial quarantine mandate. Pastors who failed to stay current with the latest updates published by the World Health Organization and their local county health departments struggled to make informed safety decisions in real time. Church members who did not respect the pandemic's severity pressured their leaders to keep the doors of the church open, not knowing that doing so could cost someone's life. The pandemic's total disruption placed stress on every aspect of our lives; we collectively suffered acute grief from the dislodging of our norms.

The pandemic made it nearly impossible for church staff to form a cohesive plan for weekly worship that could withstand the ebb and flow of pandemic living. One week, a camera person might not be available. Another week, a musician might not be available to prerecord. At times, the pastor had to rely on themselves to maintain a level of consistency on their virtual platform. The radical interruption of ministry's normal workflow consequently produced an unexpected outcome for the postquarantine church: a reclamation of ancient Christian spiritual disciplines that foster soul-care and self-care both in the lives of the pastor and the people in the pews. By soul-care, I am referring to the practice of those habits and spiritual disciplines that heal the mind, body, and soul of a person who has suffered under the perpetual onslaught of life's daily challenges. By self-care, I am referring to those attitudes and decisions that allow for the intentional planning of rest as a form of healing and spiritual renewal.

As Dr. Heatley states succinctly in his text, self-care is an essential for all—especially those who labor in the local church.[4] We pastors learned during the pandemic how easily we can fall into the habit of prioritizing the work of ministry at the expense of our commitment to self-care. It is sad to say that members of our congregations unknowingly, and sometimes knowingly, make it easy for pastors to give abundantly of themselves until there is nothing left, not realizing that pastors are finite. Just as sprinters have a limited number of races to run in their body, pastors have a limited number of sermons to preach and ministry tasks to fulfill. At some point, in the words of the great prophet Isaiah, we will all wither like grass and fade like the flower in the field (Isaiah 40:6–8). Adding to the need for self-care, I contend we need to focus on soul-care. We all need to cultivate daily habits and practices that reflect Jesus's approach to calming the fears and concerns that accompany our new reality in Gennesaret. With words, presence, and even planned moments of solitude, we need to be more intentional about embracing the God of our disruptions and leaning into the promises inherent in God's presence.

For a postquarantine church seeking to land differently on the back-side of the pandemic's storm, caring strategies can begin with intentional efforts to just sit with Jesus. One practical model for sitting with Jesus as a form of soul-care can be found at the St. John's Downtown Church in Houston, Texas, where former Pastors Rudy and Juanita Rasmus have served as the visionary founders and pastoral leaders for more than thirty years. At St. John's, physical and virtual spaces were created for grief, family, and mental health support in peer-led groups. Participants in these intimate settings can share their grief and receive support for their mental distress. As a form of soul-care, sitting with Jesus may simply mean being intentional about dwelling in God's presence in intimate spaces with pastoral counselors and grief therapists. It may mean forming healthy practices of just being with God and with one another, both virtually and

---

4. Ibid., 93.

in person, and acknowledging each other's fragility. Just sitting with Jesus—much like the disciples sat with Jesus in the boat after the storm on the Sea of Galilee—may mean openly embracing our communal need for a daily dosage of God's strength and acknowledging that we need to affirm each other's humanity. We are all created in God's image.

In addition to sitting, I believe Jesus teaches us through Mark's written account the value of communing with God and one another. Jesus didn't just sit with the disciples while the boat drifted to Gennesaret; he also communed with them. Jesus shared in the responsibility of helping the disciples to recenter their faith and to trust in the one whose sacred storms had redirected them. The postquarantine church needs to invest in more strategic and imaginative ways through which its members can forge new bonds together. We have been disrupted by the gale force winds of the pandemic and are still learning what it means to both give and receive from one another as equal partners in the work of soul rehabilitation. The dislodged and spiritually displaced are looking for a community that has a vested interest in the caring of the soul. Even though external factors compete for the attention of God's people, bold notions of what it means to be in community still exist in today's society.

What would it look like, for example, to share responsibility in helping the drug addict find a community where they can recover, or to assist the person who lost their job and has no health insurance, or to help the single mother without a familial support system? How would it look if our churches allowed their pastors to enjoy an extended sabbath rest away from the church as a holy effort to help the pastor kindle a new spiritual flame? How much stronger would our churches be if we took the time to commune with our youth who may have strayed away from the church during the pandemic and who lack the support needed to reengage their spiritual community? How much more relevant would the church be if it offered weekly grief shares for those who mourn the loss of loved ones? What if every church could offer virtual and in-person support for those who care for the elderly with dementia or struggle to find placement for the long-term care of their parents or grandparents?

All of humanity, no matter their political, religious, or socioeconomic location, experienced varying degrees of radical disruption during the pandemic. Every member of society, no matter their gender identity or sexual orientation, needs a message of hope in the midst of the unknown.

God's example through the embodiment of Jesus demonstrates the holy power of communing together during and after life's intense storms. As the prophet proclaimed in Isaiah 41:10, God dwells among us regardless of our radical disruptions, offering an assurance that the storms will not have the final say over God's intended purpose for our lives. Our God shares the responsibility in helping us reclaim our faith in an unpredictable world. When we sit with God and with one another—when we commune together—we can forge ahead in stormy weather.

Mark doesn't say so explicitly, but I can imagine Jesus assuring the disciples and letting them know that, while they may not have landed in Bethsaida, Gennesaret serves a specific purpose. The Plain of Gennesaret may be the place of the lost and weary traveler, but it can also be a place where abundant grace can be found. What would it look like if the pulpit's message was more intentional in its assurance that, despite life's turbulence, with God new beginnings are always possible? How much more relevant would our messaging be if we proclaimed a God who not only sits and communes with us but shares responsibility in helping us redefine our purpose on the backside of life's unexpected storms? Could the church begin its soul-care with a word that does not trivialize life's unexpected disruptions but rather points to a God who journeys with us through turbulence? A homiletical method that makes sense for the church today will anchor itself not in superficial inklings of a prosperity gospel but on the rock that reminds us: if we have faith, God can make a way. Jesus sits with the disciples and communes with them much in the way Grandmaster Flash & the Furious Five communed with the marginalized and oppressed while delivering "The Message" to an urban community disrupted by poverty, gun violence, and crack cocaine. I envision Jesus encouraging the disciples with each pull of the oars toward Gennesaret that the same God who fed the five thousand was there with them.

## THE WIND BLOWS TO BOSSTOWN

By the end of the tracking session in Chung King Studios, I could feel that cool breeze. Again, I began to ask myself subconsciously: "Did somebody turn the air conditioning down again? Maybe I have a summer head cold." I wasn't afforded much time to ponder the matter, as I was informed that Whodini would record their vocals in Atlanta, and I needed to pack my bags immediately. My friend Clean Cut accompanied me, and we prepared for a trip to A-Town—the New York of the South and crunk capital of the world.

Soundscape Studios in Atlanta was formed in 1985 to offer a high-tech recording space for a variety of music groups like R.E.M., the Black Crowes, Another Bad Creation, Peabo Bryson, and the Conway Brothers. By 1991, multiplatinum R&B singer Bobby Brown purchased the recording facility and renamed it Bosstown Recording Studios. Bosstown became home to major performing artists like Alyson Williams, Xscape, Kris Kross, Akon, TLC, Arrested Development, and Elton John—and it was the place where I began phase two of my recording process with Whodini. Much like Jesus sat with, communed, and assured the disciples of their safety as they headed toward Gennesaret, Clean Cut and I sat with, communed, and assured Ecstasy, Jahlil, and Grandmaster Dee that they would enjoy chart success and national acclaim in 1996 as they did in 1983.

In many regards, the hip-hop scene in Atlanta during the mid-1990s was as different from New York as Gennesaret was from Bethsaida. Gangster Rap began to give way to a new sound in the "Dirty South" pioneered by local legends DJ Smurf, MC Shy D, OutKast, Arrested Development, Goodie Mob, Organized Noize, Jermaine Dupri, and Lil Jon. This new hip-hop subgenre, eventually called "crunk," catapulted the southern region to hip-hop prominence rivaling the success of the eastern and western coastal hip-hop regions. Not only did Atlanta emerge as the Motown of the South during the mid-1990s, but Atlanta's club scene exploded as Blacks migrated from northern cities into the South. Nightclubs like Magic City, Club 559, the Gold Club, and Club Kaya became cultural incubators where professional dancers, local rappers, and singers intermingled with drug dealers, record executives, and rap luminaries. A distinct sound and culture formed quickly, separating the city of Atlanta's crunk subgenre from hip-hop movements in New York City, Philadelphia, and Los Angeles.

Arguably the most pivotal individual responsible for enhancing my education on the convergence of Atlanta's crunk and club scene was my dear colleague, brother, and friend Ricardo "Road Manager Rick" Braithwaite. Rick was the road manager of rap groups like 3rd Bass, featuring MC Serch, Pete Nice, and DJ Richie Rich. He toured the world with most of Def Jam Recordings' leading hip-hop acts in the late 1980s and early 1990s, then relocated to the city of Atlanta just prior to my arrival to produce a new song with Whodini. As youth, Rick and I had shared the same handball and basketball courts in the Crown Heights section of Brooklyn. Now on car drives together through Bankhead, West Side, and Southwest Atlanta in 1996, Rick gave me a feel for the rich texture of a budding cultural movement and the South's new sound.

One hour into the recording session with Whodini, luminaries from Atlanta began to visit the studio. First was Bobby Brown's brother Tommy, followed by representatives of Jermaine Dupri's record label So So Def Recordings. Other prominent figures from the city later joined the session to watch one of the greatest rap groups in hip-hop history in the sound booth—first Ecstasy, and then Jahlil, delivering the lyrics with poetic ease. Just like at Chung King Studios in New York City, the crowd moved rhythmically from side to side, chanting, "Jahlil . . . ah my mello my man . . . Ecstasy . . . ah my mello my man . . . Grandmaster Dee . . . ah my mello my man . . . Who-di-ni . . . rock the house!" With each succeeding chant, Ecstasy and Jahlil became even more energized in their recordings. The new beginning was at hand.

## SPACE FOR THE DISRUPTED

Historically speaking, the Black church has always functioned as a landing place for the disrupted. When white supremacists planted a bomb under the steps of the 16th Street Baptist Church in Birmingham, Alabama, in 1963, it was the efforts of church members, freedom fighters, and community activists that created a haven for the terrorized. When the Pleasant Grove Missionary Baptist Church in Rankin, Mississippi, was burned shortly before midnight in 1964, it was the labor of the faithful and their allies that created a space for the maligned to reclaim their spiritual center. When the Flood Christian Church in Ferguson, Missouri, was burned· by arsonists during a series of protests over the police shooting of Michael Brown, Jr. in 2014, it was spirit-filled activists, community organizers, and civil rights leaders who worked in tandem to create a pocket of peace where the frustrated and discouraged could reclaim their hope. When nine members of the Emanuel African Methodist Episcopal Church in Charleston, South Carolina, were murdered by a white supremacist in 2015, it was the A.M.E. Church— along with allies, networks, and grassroots organizations—who created a path of mourning, grief, and recovery in the face of fear and tyranny.

The Black church in America has been an institution through which the spirit of God has moored God's soul-restoring presence alongside the shores of a terrorized and disrupted people here. The church of today must remember to remain a spiritual oasis for the disrupted much in the way Jesus embraced the disrupted disciples at the Sea of Galilee. Jesus did and still does offer the church a pedagogy by which it can sit with, commune, and assure the hearts of the radically disrupted that God dwells among them and intends to bring them to a place of new beginnings just on the other side of their unexpected storms.

In Atlanta, places like Ebenezer Baptist Church, Wheat Street Baptist Church, Friendship Baptist Church, and Big Bethel A.M.E. Church have all served as spiritual anchors and beacons of hope to communities determined not to give into despair. Institutions like Morehouse College, Spelman College, Clark Atlanta University, and Morris Brown College have played a pivotal role in developing some of the most brilliant thought-leaders, social change advocates, and captains of industry. As was the case in New York City, in Atlanta young people in the hip-hop generation who were unchurched in the 1980s and 1990s tuned our spirits to the nontraditional urban prophets who preached their raw and uncut messages outside the traditional pulpit. Atlanta's youth population knew the disruptions of capital greed, mass incarceration, systemic racism, housing discrimination, poorly funded educational systems, fragmented family structures, and a growing voting constituency demanding a shift in the political sphere.

Underground hip-hop communities in cities like Atlanta have also produced the likes of Raheem the Dream, Mojo, Hitman Sammy Sam, Kilo Ali, Big Boi, André 3000, Ludacris, and T.I. During the 1980s, 1990s, and early 2000s, these hip-hop luminaries helped an unchurched youth population discern the winds of change through poetic proclamations, economic boycotts, and community gatherings. Thus, an alternative ideological framework and worldview was cultivated for youth looking to reimagine their sense of identity. The hip-hop movement in the South helped this younger generation formulate a newly empowered Black body politic representing their social and political interests. For example, had it not been for the establishment of grassroots organizations like the Hip-Hop Summit Action Network (co-founded by Russell Simmons and Dr. Benjamin Chavis), identifying Black political talent and consolidating political interests in urban centers would have been far more difficult. The Hip-Hop Summit Action Network—a nonprofit, nonpartisan national coalition of hip-hop artists, entertainment industry leaders, education advocates, and civil rights activists—partnered with the Black church and other community grassroots organizations to help rally the vote that led to the ascension of national leaders like President Barack Obama and the Rev. Dr. Senator Raphael Warnock.

As a cultural movement, hip-hop has always had its pews filled with those who have experienced radical disruptions and gale force winds. It can even be argued that the hip-hop movement offers the same essential components that make the church what we know to be the church. Hip-hop offers an "MC" who proclaims the word, a "DJ" who functions like a worship leader, a graffiti artist who functions like a scribe, and even

"Break-dancers" or "Crunk-dancers" who function like gifted liturgical artists. More importantly, hip-hop offers its members a sense of belonging through a common experience, through which a transcendent form of consciousness arises. It is because of hip-hop that we have the Hip-Hop Caucus, a nonprofit organization aiming to promote political activism for young US voters using hip-hop music and culture. The evolution of hip-hop as both a musical genre and cultural movement has led to the creation of think-tanks like Rock the Vote, which teaches urban youth about the value of freedom of speech and the political power gained through full democratic participation. Hip-hop has given birth to organizations like Hip-Hop for Change, Inc., which focuses on self-empowerment, consolidating political interests at the local level to build businesses, control politics, and allocate financial resources at the municipal and county level. The organization also emphasizes the importance of building an economic base within the entertainment industry to take back the ownership of what hip-hop has meant to the communities it originated from.

While it's true that much of hip-hop has been co-opted by corporate greed, self-aggrandizement, toxic masculinity, and unfettered capitalism, it's also true that the church wrestles with many of the same economic barriers, narcissistic behaviors, and social-cultural challenges. One could argue that hip-hop in its original form has always been an open and embracing community, much like the early Christian church when it was at its best. In a stark contrast to the church, however, hip-hop communities have been less interested in assimilating into dominant culture or ascribing to a modern Western European view of success, sexuality, or a sense of self-worth in ways largely adopted by the historical Black church and other social institutions within the Black community. If being a part of the church means dehumanizing those who do not share the same life experiences as those in the church, the masses will continue to seek other alternative communities, like hip-hop, to be authentically affirmed in their humanity.

As a byproduct of hip-hop culture myself, I must inform the church that there are hip-hop communities both within the United States and across the globe that offer strong religious traditions, their own code of ethics, a distinct communal sense of belonging, and the same form of genuine love you would hope to find in any Christian congregation. In many regards, hip-hop arose among youth as a response to a church that failed to listen to their pain, struggles, and aspirations. The church of today must not underestimate these hip-hop communities or the new emerging grassroots movements that offer a sense of community not always found in the traditional sanctuary. These emerging communities are mostly driven by Millennials and Gen Z, who desire spirituality without the traditional moorings of organized religion, to provide an alternative form of transcendent consciousness. The church is not the only game in town and has not been for more than sixty years. To millions of youth across the globe, hip-hop in its purest form offers a sense of moral grounding, messaging, and shelter without the elements of patriarchy, sexism, and gender discrimination that continue to run rampant in the postmodern church.

To engage in caring strategies, to support the disrupted as they reflect on how to land differently after a storm, the church today must sit with, commune, and assure these people that God dwells among them—just like Jesus sat with and assured the disciples. Today's preachers cannot be afraid to proclaim with hip-hop rhythm that God still offers hope in a land gripped by the gale force winds of fear, greed, anxiety, and despair. On the Sea of Galilee, Jesus offered a hip-hop model of leadership that the postquarantine church and the disrupted of today can still use to find a sense of purpose and mission. Mark's Gospel reminds the reader that, when Jesus is present, the opportunity for a new beginning in the middle of unsettling change is always possible.

## LIVING INTO THE EBB AND FLOW

Within a month's time after my recording session with Whodini at Bosstown Recordings, the rap group returned to New York City to begin recording a video for their soon-to-be-released lead single, "Keep Running Back," produced by Jermaine Dupri and Carl So-Lowe. Video producers, directors, record executives, professional models, recording artists, and their guests flooded a condo on the Lower East Side of Manhattan—famously known as Marcus Graham's bachelor pad from the movie *Boomerang*—where director Reginald Hudlin filmed a large portion of the footage for Whodini's new music video.

Arriving at the site was like entering into a perfect convergence of amazing talent from both the North and the South. Artists from So So Def Recordings like Kriss Kross and Da Brat intermingled with artists from Def Jam Recordings and producers like Spyderman and me. In between conversations could be heard the words "Action!" followed by "Cut!" Miles of wiring covered the floor, while the lighting on set was constantly being readjusted to create the perfect shot. On the side, makeup artists powdered the face of singer-songwriter Trey Lorenz, who was featured on Mariah Carey's cover of "I'll Be There," the 1970 number one Jackson Five single. When the makeup artists were not working on Trey's face and neck, they were adjusting his white leisure suit and complementing black silk shirt.

In one particular scene for the video, Trey sang the hook to the song while on a manufactured ledge just outside the condo. As he continued to sing the hook, originally written and produced by Jimmy Jam & Terry Lewis on the Cherrelle R&B hit "Everything I Miss at Home," I felt the cool breeze again. The momentum of the breeze intensified slightly, just enough to let me know that what had joined me in Orlando followed me to Atlanta and now to this condo on the Lower Eastside of Manhattan. As I made small talk with other artists and executives whom I befriended through mutual acquaintances in the recording industry, I could feel the ebb and flow of the breeze. I asked myself again, "Am I coming down with something?" I couldn't ignore it. I asked Ecstasy in between a scene, "Yo, Ecs . . . do you feel that?"

## BLOWN AWAY FROM DANGER

As the filming of the Whodini video continued into the night and early the following morning, I received a text from another acquaintance in the recording industry. The acquaintance had an incredible opportunity to present, and I needed to meet with them the following afternoon. I agreed, and we met in a conference room of a record label in downtown Manhattan. My acquaintance asked me to sit back and listen to a demo he received from an amateur talent. Within twenty seconds, I recognized that what I was listening was a hit. For those of us who produce records, we know a hit when we hear one. This particular R&B song, which had been produced over a commonly known break beat from the Incredible Bongo Band's "Apache," grabbed you from the very start. This was a fail-proof demo.

"What do you want me to do with the record?" I asked.

"I want to do this song over with you as the producer."

"How is that possible when the song is so distinct?" I argued. "Whoever made this record will know they sent their demo to you. The moment you get a record company to release this song, the person who produced this record will sue both you and the record company!"

"I don't think you understand. I already have a commitment in the form of a contract from a record company to reproduce this song under the condition that you agree to reproduce it for them. They are offering to let you keep all of your publishing. They've also offered me an executive producer credit and a new job as A&R over their R&B division." I could feel the breeze as he continued. "In fact, the CEO and his current head of A&R have agreed to come meet with you right now."

"Say what?"

"They should be here momentarily," he said. "When I told them that Chris Large agreed to take the meeting, they said they had to be here."

Just as he finished speaking, the CEO and head of A&R walked into the meeting room. "Chris, we just want you to know that we are glad you decided to take this meeting," the CEO said. "We recognize that this isn't a typical business meeting you are accustomed to, but we think there is a lot of money to be made here. We think you can help us break a once-in-a-lifetime kind of record."

"Do you realize that I did not produce this original demo? Someone else produced this song!"

The CEO responded, "We are well aware where the demo came from. That doesn't matter to us. Your acquaintance suggested to us that you would be interested in reproducing this song. We'll provide the singer. We just need you to reproduce the track."

From that moment on, I couldn't recall anything else being mentioned in the meeting. That cool subtle breeze suddenly turned into a gale force wind, muffling the words of the executives who were speaking in the meeting. The wind only calmed down enough for me to give my final response:

"If I were to produce this record, I would never be able to regain my integrity as a producer. My career would be over before it ever got started." I concluded the meeting by saying, "I am afraid you are going to have to find someone else to reproduce that song. I can't do it. It just doesn't sit right with me."

Six months later, that song climbed into the top ten on the R&B charts. I never heard from that acquaintance again. As I left the room, the forceful wind subsided to a calm breeze. I walked into the elevator saying to myself, "I definitely need to see a doctor. I can't seem to shake this chill. No matter where I go, it's always there."

## HOW TO LAND WELL IN OUR GENNESARET

Life's unexpected events are common to the human experience. No matter our age, life has a way of redirecting our plans and reordering our steps. American history is filled with accounts of people who set out to accomplish one feat only to be redirected toward accomplishing another. There are scores of historic moments when a tragic event or an unexpected test of moral character pushed a community to make decisions they otherwise would not have considered.

For instance, the brutal killing of Trayvon Benjamin Martin in 2012, savagely gunned down by twenty-eight-year-old vigilante George Zimmerman, led to the massive mobilization of grassroots organizations, churches, and hip-hop advocacy groups aimed at protesting the moral debasement of "Stand Your Ground" laws. Rallies swelled all over the

United States in protest after a jury acquitted Zimmerman of second-degree murder and manslaughter. One of the unanticipated outcomes of this national tragedy was the emergence of Trayvon's mother, Sybrina Fulton, as a prominent voice in the fight for social equity and the leader of the Mothers of the Movement—a group of women whose black children were killed by police officers or gun violence. Sybrina Fulton did not set out to become one of the leading activists in the world prior to the demise of her beloved son. Emmett Till's mother, Mamie Elizabeth Till-Mobley, did not set out personally to confront the death-dealing practices of lynching in the South prior to the tragic murder of her own fourteen-year-old son. Samaria Rice did not set out to advocate for juvenile rights prior to the public execution of her twelve-year-old son Tamir Rice at the hand of a police officer. However, Sybrina, Mamie, Samaria, and countless Black mothers like them made a conscious decision to confront the systems of oppression and the cultural norms strangling the life out of Black boys all over the United States. Mothers of the Movement commits itself to raising awareness of the pervasiveness of racism within the law enforcement community in the United States, and they offer caring strategies for families and communities who have been forced to land differently on the backside of Black death. They discuss life after loss, how to manage grief, and how to move forward after a traumatic event.

Hip-hop offers its own examples of individuals who courageously reimagined what it meant to live in their own Gennesaret, using the disruptive winds of change for their good rather than their destruction. Take, for instance, the acclaimed rapper Cardi B: Recognized by *Forbes* as one of the most influential female rappers of all time, Cardi B started as a dancer at a strip club in Tribeca, New York, at the age of eighteen—a job that provided her the means to attend Manhattan Borough Community College and escape poverty and a physically violent relationship. In 2015, Cardi B joined the cast of the VH1 reality television series *Love & Hip Hop: New York*. The following year, in 2016, Cardi B was featured in her first endorsement deal with Romantic Depot, and in 2017, Cardi B signed her first major record label recording contract with Atlantic Records. On June 16, 2017, Atlantic Records released Cardi B's commercial debut single, "Bodak Yellow." After the release of her debut studio album, *Invasion of Privacy*, in 2018, Cardi B became the first female artist to win the Grammy Award for Best Rap Album as a solo artist.

While many continue to critique Cardi B for what some perceive to be an overly hypersexual expression of art in music form, I contend Cardi B navigated the disrupting storms of poverty and domestic violence, adjusting to a new course rather than succumbing to the winds. Cardi B tapped into her lived experience and monetized a unique form of artistic expression, vulgar as it may be to some, so that she would land differently in Gennesaret. The rapper Meg the Stallion joins Cardi B and other female rappers who were born into social dynamics beyond their control and yet reached into the depths of their creative genius to reimagine what it could mean to live in Gennesaret on their own terms. For such hip-hop artists, radical disruption does not have to equate to total destruction. To the contrary, radical disruption can offer an opportunity to experience life in a different way.

If you believe Jesus to be omniscient, Mark's Gospel does not make it easy for to explain why Jesus sent the disciples to Bethsaida if he knew they would land in Gennesaret. Many of us would make the case that we never intended to land in the place where we find ourselves now. Some of us have survived the storm of a child's unexpected death. We have navigated the aftermath of a failed marriage. We have been diagnosed with a terminal illness. We have a child who has chosen a path that stands in direct conflict with the values we taught them when they were young. We have been passed over for a promotion because of age, gender, race, or political preference. Perhaps we have become disgruntled with circumstances beyond our control.

I contend that if we read the sixth chapter in Mark's Gospel closely, we can find the one who is able to help us deal with life's harsh and demoralizing storms. And although knowing that Jesus is with us doesn't necessarily make our daily decisions any easier, I believe we can firmly hold on to the hope that there is life after the storm when we remember that Jesus is truly present for the duration of our life's journey. Gennesaret was a land of the displaced and the wayfarer. The disciples never intended to land there, yet Jesus's caring presence through the storm prepared them for the time spent in Gennesaret. I believe the postquarantine church can have the same effect on those who walk through the church's physical and virtual doors if members become more intentional about sitting, communing, and assuring the hearts of the disrupted that there really is life to be lived and purpose to be found in the place of the unexpected.

# 6

## VESTIGES OF HOPE IN A POSTQUARANTINE WORLD

*When they got out of the boat, people at once
recognized him, and rushed about that whole region
and began to bring the sick on mats to wherever
they heard he was.*

**—Mark 6:54–55**

In September 1994, I received a call from one of the managers investing in my future career as a producer at the time. He explained that he thought it would be a good idea to travel to Pleasantville, New Jersey, to meet a young up-and-coming R&B producer who shared a similar trajectory as my own. This young producer was Rodney "Darkchild" Jerkins. Rodney became known for producing hits like "Don't Wanna Be a Player" featuring Joe, "The Boy Is Mine" featuring Brandy and Monica, "I Can Love You" featuring Mary J. Blige and Lil' Kim, "Oops! . . . I Did It Again" featuring Britney Spears, "Unbreakable" featuring Michael Jackson and The Notorious B.I.G., and "Déjà Vu" featuring Beyoncé—just to name a few. At the time, Rodney had already begun rendering remixes for artists on Bad Boy Entertainment and Uptown

Records/MCA. The word circulating through the industry rumor mill at the time was that Rodney was a child prodigy. He was considered one of the stellar music producers who would change the tone and tenor of the music industry for years to come. My handlers suggested making the connection could possibly lead to future ventures.

It just so happened that an acquaintance of Rodney's took a temporary residence in the Panorama City townhouse where Brett B., Spyderman, other producers, and I often gathered to create music. Raul "Freaknasti" Santiago had a relationship with Rodney and offered to facilitate a meeting at Rodney's home in Pleasantville. Raul produced the lead single "Posse (Shoot 'Em Up)" featuring the rapper Intelligent Hoodlum for the soundtrack to the Mario Van Peebles–directed movie *Posse*. I agreed to go with Raul to meet the young man who many suggested was well on his way in the industry.

After flying from Los Angeles back to New Jersey, the person who met Raul and me at the Atlantic City bus depot was Rodney's father, Rev. Frederick Jerkins. Raul explained to me that Rev. Jerkins was also Rodney's business manager. Rev. Jerkins took meticulous care of Rodney to ensure that his time and focus were properly accounted for. As the old adage goes, time (literally) is money. Rev. Jerkins picked us up in a gold Mercedes-Benz and drove us to the Jerkins' home. Mrs. Jerkins met us at the door and greeted us warmly. I was not a churchgoer at the time, but if I went to church, I would have equated the Jerkins household to visiting a friendly congregation. The only other home I knew that offered this kind of Christian hospitality was the home of the Clean Cut Craig and his family in Brooklyn. There was a buzz in the two-level Jerkins home, and those who were there talked about the goodness of the Lord in between vibrant discussions about all the wonderful remix opportunities on the table for Rodney.

After engaging in a few more pleasantries with Reverend and Mrs. Jerkins, I was escorted to the lower level where Rodney was waiting for us. Rodney was a studio in the lower level where he spent a considerable portion of his time working on preproduction prior to the shopping of his own creative material. After Raul introduced me to Rodney, Rodney suggested that he was looking to upgrade his catalog of percussion sounds and asked me to show him what I had in my repertoire. I proceeded to upload several drum sounds from my own MPC-60 II floppy disks. The first drum sequence I produced in Rodney's basement would eventually be used on the single "Head Nod," featuring the rapper Hodge for the soundtrack to the original motion picture *Panther*. Rodney, Raul, and I collaborated to co-produce and write most of the lyrics to the song. I distinctly remember reciting, "And all my thanks . . . it goes to God . . . for giving me the chance to make my head nod." This closing line arose within my consciousness specifically because of my awareness being in a Christian home. The Jerkins household offered my first exposure to the possibility of a bridge between the secular and the church. Rodney and Bruce Carbone at Mercury Records eventually remixed the song using musical elements of the R&B group Tony! Toni! Toné!'s recording, "Anniversary."

## BREAKING THROUGH WITH NAS

While uploading and creating different drum sequences in Rodney's basement, a new opportunity came through my management team. It was brought to my attention that filming for the movie *Street Fighter* had been recently completed. Corporate executives at Capcom had decided to create a soundtrack to accompany the release of this new action film. Featuring popular martial artist Jean-Claude Van Damme and directed by Steven E. de Souza, the film was based on a 1987 one-on-one video game of the same name. By 1994 when the film was released, the video game had amassed over $4 billion in units sold worldwide. The soundtrack included artists like the Pharcyde, MC Hammer, Deion Sanders, Craig Mack, Ice Cube, LL Cool J, the Wreck League, Public Enemy, Paris, and Another Level. One of the final artists to be considered for the soundtrack was Columbia Records' new recording artist, Nas. The original producer slated to record a song with Nas for the soundtrack was not available, and Nas needed to find another producer in time to make the deadline for the movie soundtrack. Raul, who had a relationship with Nas's personal business manager, agreed with my managers that this was a career-defining opportunity.

Nas was considered within the hip-hop industry to be the hottest lyricist on the planet. To some, Nas represented the best lyrical convergence of genius rappers like Rakim and Kool G Rap. His debut album, *Illmatic*, received universal acclaim, and it was considered the best album of the year—and arguably the greatest hip-hop album of all time. Famous beatmakers like Q-Tip, Pete Rock, DJ Premier, Large Professor, and L.E.S were all contributors to *Illmatic*, which was eventually inducted into the Library of Congress's National Recording Registry. Singles like "The World Is Yours," "It Ain't Hard to Tell," "Halftime," and "One Love" captured the heart, struggles, and aspirations of a resilient youth culture who used every resource at their disposal to survive the labyrinth of challenges commonly experienced in the city streets of New York.

In many regards, Nas was considered more than a poetic sage from Queensbridge. He was the full embodiment of the youth in cities like New York City, Philadelphia, and Chicago who used hip-hop as a vehicle to express their dreams and rage in the face of a sociopolitical system that failed to meet their basic needs. These failures were often intentionally legislated to deprive certain populations in the inner city of a decent quality of life. Queensbridge became an incubator for talents like Marley Marl, MC Shan, Cormega, Tragedy Khadafi, Big Noyd, Havoc, Craig G, and Roxanne Shanté. Many of the artists and producers who were reared in this section of Long Island City used their genius creative abilities to paint a picture through words and rhythmic musical compositions to convey the struggles of coping with being young and gifted in an underfunded concrete jungle.

For those of us raised in New York City hip-hop culture, Nas also represented a strong response to new voices from other markets throughout the country who were releasing their own contextualized version of a hip-hop sound. Organized Konfusion released *Stress: The Extinction Agenda*, Outkast released *Southernplayalisticadillacmuz*, Scarface released *The Diary*, and Warren G. released *Regulate . . . G Funk Era* as examples of hip-hop taking root in markets not dominated by rappers from the east coast. For hardcore hip-hop fans from the northeast, Nas was the ultimate hip-hop lyricist and embodied the best of boom bap rap. *Illmatic* was believed to be the gold standard by which all albums should be compared. Messages had been sent throughout the industry that no one else should ever expect to work with Nas if they were not a member of the original stable of producers on *Illmatic*.

This was the Nas who walked into Greene St. Recording Studios in SoHo, Manhattan, in late October 1994. The explicit instructions I had been given from both my management and Nas's business manager was that I had one shot to play a selection of instrumentals when Nas arrived. If he liked a track, he would stay for the entire session. If not, he would walk out of the studio. In fairness to Nas, he had established himself with a very specific sound; it was understandable why he would be apprehensive to record on a track that was sonically inconsistent with his body of work thus far. After listening to a few of my first selections, it was clear that Nas did not like any of the tracks I had played up to that point. We then reached what I considered the best section of my cassette tape. If Nas was going to select a track to work with, it would surely be one of the selections recorded on this portion of the tape. By the grace of God, Nas selected an instrumental that I had created in Los Angeles four months prior at Greene St. Recording Studio. The track borrowed elements from the jazz pianist Ahmad Jamal's *The Awakening*.

After choosing a track, Nas told everyone in the room that he needed to leave and that he would return shortly. Nas's manager, myself, and Raul, who was also present at this recording session because of his close relationship with Nas's manager, looked at one another as if we might have all been had. Raul and I walked outside the studio and saw Nas drive off in a Montero jeep. I wondered if my once-in-a-lifetime opportunity had passed.

Fortunately, Nas returned, along with his brother "Jungle." Nas asked for a pen and pad, and then proceeded to write what I believe to be one of the classic unheralded rhymes in the Nas catalog. In less than an hour,

Nas wrote his entire song and suggested that he was ready to record. Nas began to recite his rhymes through the thousand-dollar microphone in the recording booth. He recorded all of his bars in one take. Nas then described how he envisioned adding combative engagements on the hook and in the end of the song to make the record more consistent with the theme and feel of the *Street Fighter* movie. Jungle, Raul, my former group mate Craig Live, my father, and I filled in gaps in the song with combative chatter to simulate what Nas envisioned on the record. I later added Craig Live to infuse a melodic vibe on the hook.

In less than twenty-four hours, I finally broke into the music industry, recording my very first record with the hottest MC in the game. Nas's decision that night at Greene St. Recording Studios, in the presence of movie executives from Universal Pictures, opened the door for Chris Large. Nas legitimized the beginning of my career as a professional music producer in the recording industry. Without the investments made by Ricky "Road Manager Rick" Braithwaite, D-Moet, Brett B., Spyderman, Johnny Pump, Hassan "Sonny" Pore, and my management team at the time, I would not have been in position to take advantage of the opportunity Raul brought to the table. Breaking into the industry with Nas in October 1994 radically shifted my life and accelerated my career as a music producer.

## WHEN THEY SAW JESUS

The Gospel of Mark's overarching message is one of a messiah, namely Jesus, whose life and activity represented the coming reign of God. Mark's message was transported westward toward Rome with the intent of making the story of Jesus compelling to a more secular and Latinized population. Mark's written accounts of Jesus interacting with non-Jewish populations and embodying the inbreaking power of God provided examples of Mark's understanding of who Jesus was and what he meant to those not raised in the villages of Galilee. In describing the scenes of Jesus casting down demons, healing the sick, calming storms, and raising the dead back to life, the Gospel of Mark invoked theological questions for his readers: How should followers of Jesus live in a world controlled by Rome, the ruling elite, and a power-hungry priestly community? Whose side should the followers in the Latinized world take when confronted with the disruptive power of the gospel? Should they "give unto Caesar," or should they continue to "give unto God?" Should they yield to Jesus's radically disruptive power or remain submitted to the brutal governance of the Roman empire? The Gospel of Mark believed that Jesus's life-giving activity among the villages of Galilee had implications for the early Christian communities of first-century Rome. Those same activities continue to have consequences today for those who desire to trust in the one who proclaimed that God's reign is near.

This soul-restoring, death-defying Jesus was quickly recognized by the people of Gennesaret when he disembarked from the boat. In contrast to the rejection he experienced in Nazareth (Mark 6:1–6), Jesus was well received by a population of people who heard about his teaching power or experienced it personally during other healing events recorded earlier in Mark's Gospel (1:32–34; 3:7–12). Mark reports that Jesus's primary function in the Gennesaret region was that of supernatural healer. The Gospel writer goes so far as to make the powerful suggestion that Jesus in Gennesaret achieves a 100 percent medical success rate: "All who touched Jesus's cloak were healed" (Mark 6:56). On the Plain in Gennesaret, Jesus is the focus of everyone's attention. Faith is found to be in abundance in a place where many have been disrupted and displaced by unexpected events.

The people in Gennesaret "saw" Jesus and believed he could heal them. One must wrestle with the contrast between the disciples who, in the midst of their storm, were not able to recognize Jesus, and the people of Gennesaret knowing Jesus as soon as he disembarked from the boat. Why couldn't the disciples recognize Jesus? Could it be that their close proximity to Jesus did not guarantee a secured faith within their own hearts? Could it be that witnessing a miracle performed for others did not necessarily translate to the willingness to submit to Jesus's authority and receive a miracle for themselves? The people in Gennesaret recognized

Jesus immediately; in so doing, the faith of the masses was activated, allowing Jesus to work his supernatural power among a people who desired to be healed.

In our close reading of Mark's account, we might also consider that Jesus was easily detected by the people on land because of his calming presence in the boat. Prior to Jesus entering into the boat, the disciples were gripped in fear and frustration by a storm they did not anticipate. However, after Jesus calmed the storm and joined the disciples in the boat, no degree of frustration or rage could take center stage in the presence of the one with power over the laws of nature. Maybe the disciples' experience in the storm humbled them to the degree that what mattered most once they landed at Gennesaret was Jesus being made visible over their own lack of faith and understanding. Meekness has a way of creating space for the divine power of God to be detected in a land filled with uncertainty or despair. Perhaps, after being reminded that Jesus had power over their unexpected storm, the disciples sat in humility waiting for Jesus to take the lead.

Wrestling with these sorts of questions should lead the church to deeper inquiry regarding what the masses see when they encounter the church. Do the people see Jesus? Or do they only see the fear, worry, and doubt of those who profess Jesus as Lord? When the disrupted, the anxious, and the displaced visit our churches for an authentic encounter with God, do they experience the calming presence of Christ? Or are they only subjected to dogma and other forms of a shallow faith that lack the evidence of a personal encounter with Jesus? Do the masses recognize Jesus in our sermons and worship services? Do they glimpse Jesus in our Sunday school classes, our digital platforms, and our community outreach initiatives? Is Jesus easily detected in children's ministries or youth gatherings? Can our own church members find Jesus in our board meetings, fellowship initiatives, and our annual church conferences? Mark challenges his reading audience with the notion that a follower can claim to be in relationship with Jesus and still not be able to detect him when life gets hard. Close proximity does not equate to faith. One must truly know Jesus to be impacted by his power. Mark's Gospel also drives home the point that the essential aim of the church should be to allow Jesus to be found. Why did the masses in Gennesaret detect Jesus so easily? I contend it was because the disciples had been humbled by the storm and intended to stay out of the way.

## RECOGNIZING JESUS IN THE CHURCH TODAY

How does the church practice the humility of discipleship so that Jesus is recognized? What actually makes the church the church, and how do we know we are looking at it when we see it?

- To begin with, the witness of a Resurrected Christ is an essential message and mooring of the Christian church. There is no replacement for a firsthand experience of the one in whom the church finds its spiritual anchoring, purpose, and mission. Our proclamation of the good news (*kerygma*) is that, in Jesus Christ, the reign of God has finally arrived. On the day of Pentecost, Peter addressed a crowd in Jerusalem and reminded them that the life, death, burial, resurrection of Jesus had been foretold by the prophet Joel (Acts 2:14–21). Not only had it been foretold, but the people gathered in Jerusalem that day had firsthand experience of these events.

- Second, the church's life should include worship (*liturgia*), the intentional practice of responding to God as the chief celebrant of life, the one who invites all people from all walks of life to gather in God's presence where each contributes their respective gifts for community (Hebrews 13:15). In such gatherings, only the Holy One can take center stage, therefore in humility each worshiper is considered a sibling in Christ, sharing a common life of faith through which they are conformed to Christ by the mysterious power of the Holy Spirit.

- Third, as a direct consequence of *kerygma* and *liturgia*, a Christian community bears evidence of Christian love and belonging (koinonia) as Jesus so commanded (John 13:34). In the church, the common currency of God's love teaches its members to practice loving their neighbors, strangers, and even their enemies through hospitality, acceptance, compassion, forgiveness, and reconciliation.

- Fourth, the church demonstrates ongoing discipleship through teaching (*didache*) followers the way of Jesus Christ. When Paul wrote to the church in Ephesus, Paul didn't speak of them learning about Christ. Instead, Paul spoke of "learning Christ" (Ephesians 4:20), much in the same way one would learn a new language when moving to a country foreign to them.

- Fifth, the church and its members must share their firsthand experience of love in an outward witness (*marturia*). The church of the New Testament must bear witness to what Christ has done in the past, present, and future, not merely for the sake of proclamation but for the desire that other people might know the same peace, joy, and love that comes with a relationship with Christ (1 Peter 3:15).

- Finally, when people look at the church, they should find within it evidence of Christian service (*diakonia*). When Jesus washed the feet of his disciples, he demonstrated what selfless love looks like in the eyes of God (John 13:5). *Diakonia* is not an individual act but a communal one; every member of the church should be encouraged to engage in activities, actions, and ministries that service the needs of the poor, the broken, the underserved, and the disrupted (Acts 6:1–6).

When Jesus can be recognized in a church that is committed to service, hope arises. When a church shows evidence of a consistent commitment to humble witness, powerful teaching, authentic worship, and genuine love, Jesus is more easily detected and the power of God is more readily experienced. The challenge of the modern church, especially as it considers how best to land from the COVID-19 storm, is to reimagine ways of forming a community (*ecclesia*) where the essential and distinctive characteristics of God's realm in Christ can be found. The creative use of technology, the infusing of dynamic forms of communication, the multiplatform ministry will remain integral parts of the postquarantine church if it intends to remain connected to its members. However, none of these mechanisms will matter if the church isn't committed to the ministry of service that is rooted in the love ethic of Jesus.

The people of Gennesaret were able to see Jesus because he came with the sole intent to serve. One must consider whether the church should be seen in the spaces where elected officials actively legislate against a woman's right to self-agency. We have to ponder how the church should show up in those spaces where gun lobbyists double down on their commitment to sell guns at the expense of our innocent children and educators. We must question whether the church is visible in those hidden chambers where delusional policymakers legislate bills that prohibit teaching on the historical contributions of communities of color. Where was the church when the governor of Texas sent two busloads of migrants to the doorstep of the vice president in Washington, DC, without warning or recourse? Where was the church when politicians in Madison, Wisconsin, presented gun legislation allowing eighteen-year-old high school students to carry firearms on school property?

To serve as Jesus did requires a transcendent form of humility that allows the servant to bow down at the feet of the weary traveler. When Jesus washed the feet of the disciples just moments prior to his arrest and crucifixion, Jesus put the concerns of his disciples over his own concern for himself. Much in the same way, when Jesus showed up at the shore of Gennesaret, he taught the disciples yet again that service arises from humility and deep compassion. When the masses saw Jesus, they believed that the power of God drew near. Hope multiplies when selfless love demonstrates itself and sets itself apart from the superficial love more commonly experienced in this world.

## VISIBLE MODELS OF SERVANT LEADERSHIP

American history records countless models of the type of servant leadership Jesus demonstrated on the Sea of Galilee and in region of Gennesaret. In many instances, those historical examples of a Christlike love ethic are found more powerfully outside the four walls of the church than within it. One such example of servant leadership was modeled at the Greensboro, North Carolina, sit-in that began on February 1, 1960. The nonviolent protest against a segregated lunch counter was organized by Ezell Blair Jr., Franklin McCain, Joseph McNeil, and David Richmond—all African American college students at North Carolina Agricultural & Technical College in Greensboro—with the aid of Ralph Johns, a local white businessman who was sympathetic to their cause. Influenced by the nonviolent protest techniques of Mahatma Gandhi and the Journey of Reconciliation, the "Greensboro Four" drew national attention to the pervasiveness of racial segregation in the Deep South. In the dining area of the Woolworth's general merchandise store, where Blacks were relegated to a standing snack bar and the lunch counter was designated for whites only, the Greensboro Four sat down at the counter and politely requested service. They remained seated as their food orders were adamantly refused by the waitstaff. The lunch counter manager contacted the local police, not knowing that Ralph Johns had already alerted the local media. The Greensboro police arrived, as did the media. A photo of the Greensboro Four appeared in local newspapers, and the protest quickly began to expand. The entire nation was able to witness a love ethic of servant leadership that denied personal comfort for the sake of confronting an entrenched system of oppression.

The following day, the Greensboro Four returned to the Woolworth's lunch counter, accompanied by an additional thirty African American college students. The group of college students sat at the Woolworth's counter from 11:00 A.M. until 3:00 P.M., quietly sitting unserved while being attacked by overly aggressive white patrons. The next day, sixty additional college students joined the protest; the day after that, nearly three hundred. Each day saw new refusals, new threats of violence, and mass arrests. By the end of February, sit-ins had spread to more than thirty cities in eight more states. At each site, protestors filled virtually every available seat, spilling out of multiple department stores and onto the sidewalk outside. When the sit-ins ended on July 26, 1960, with the desegregation of the Woolworth's counters and those in dining facilities across the South, more than seventy thousand people had participated in sit-ins across the country. The Greensboro sit-ins provided a template for how servant leadership can restore the humanity of the underserved. The Greensboro Four sat with, communed, and assured the hearts of the people they represented at the Woolworth's lunch counter, much like Jesus did on the Sea of Galilee. Through their act of courageous non-violent protest, the love ethic of Jesus was seen, and, like in the land of Gennesaret, hope began to rise.

On August 9, 2014, an eighteen-year-old African American male named Michael Brown was shot and killed by police officer Darren Wilson in Ferguson, Missouri, a suburb of St. Louis. As the *Los Angeles Times* reported, Michael Brown's twenty-two-year-old friend Dorian Johnson contradicted Wilson's account of the events prior to the shooting.[1] Wilson, a white male police officer, said an altercation ensued when Brown attacked him in his police vehicle. Johnson said Wilson initiated the confrontation by grabbing Brown through his patrol car window, threatening Brown, and then shooting at him. According to Officer Wilson, Michael Brown stopped and charged at him after a short pursuit. According to Dorian Johnson, Brown turned around with his hands raised after Wilson shot at his back. In the entire altercation, Wilson fired a total of twelve bullets; Brown was struck six times, all in the front of his body.[2]

In response to the tragic killing of Michael Brown, protestors and justice advocates from across the country rallied in Ferguson, armed with simple yet poignant messages: "Black lives matter," "Hands up, don't shoot."[3] In addition to the public protests, organizers in Ferguson led discussions on

---

1. Matt Pierce, "BackStory: What Happened in Michael Brown Shooting in Ferguson, Mo.?" November 24, 2014, *Los Angeles Times*, https://www.latimes.com/nation/la-na-back-story-ferguson-shooting-story.html.

2. Ibid.

3. Charlotte Alter, "St. Louis Cops Condemn Rams' 'Hands Up, Don't Shoot' Gesture," *Time*, December 1, 2014.

how local communities can practice their own models of leadership to combat racism and systemic injustice. It was because of the servant leadership demonstrated in Ferguson that the FBI announced the following Monday its intentions to create the first federal database on arrest-related fatalities. It was because of the love ethic undergirding the chant "Black lives matter" that a national discussion developed concerning how race and inherent biases can influence methods of policing in America. The deaths of John Crawford III, Tamir Rice, Sandra Bland, and Freddie Gray all followed the killing of Michael Brown and became major news stories because of the social justice advocates and grassroots community organizers who worked to expose the deadly correlation between race and police brutality. Advocacy movements in places like Ferguson, Louisville, Baltimore, and Sacramento helped a broader constituency understand the cycle between systemic racism, poor police training, and the higher rate of incarceration and death among Black communities in America.

Many unsung heroes, historical figures, and entire communities have modeled the compassion of Jesus at different points in history. Moreover, countless youth and young adults within the Black and Brown communities have played a large role in liberating their people from many of America's unjust practices. Our younger generations have taught us that, when the character of Jesus can be found, hope usually arises among the disrupted. As long as the masses can see the compassionate work of Jesus, they will come running toward him. This model of servant leadership is not contingent upon membership in any particular congregation. One does not need to claim an affiliation with the Progressive National Baptist Convention, the Church of God in Christ, or the Presbyterian Church (USA) to be able to render the kind of selfless love Jesus readily shared in the land of Gennesaret. What matters most is that an individual has the capacity to recognize the humanity of others. A person's faith is strengthened exponentially when the incarnate presence of Christ is found through acts of service.

Jesus performed miracles throughout the region of Gennesaret because the masses recognized him and believed he had the power to heal them. One's faith in the God who heals can grow exponentially if one is led to believe that God is accessible. May our youth and young adults continue to teach us that God has the power to heal through the mind, hands, and feet of those who have a mind to serve.

## THE FORCE OF THE WIND

I can remember learning in class that the force of wind is calculated using the mass of air and the acceleration of wind. The average density of air at sea level is approximately 1.229 kilograms per cubic meter. The area the wind hits is measured in square meters. The mass of air hitting a surface then equals air density times area. The acceleration (a) equals the square of the wind speed in meters per second (m/s). Using the formula force (F) equals mass (m) times acceleration (a), one can then calculate the wind force in Newtons (N). One Newton equals one kilogram-meter per second squared. I cannot tell you the mass or acceleration of wind that grabbed hold of my musical career upon the completion of the record "One on One" that I produced for Nas to be featured on the *Street Fighter* movie soundtrack. What I can tell you is that the force was massive. Anytime a producer is privileged to work with a platinum artist, nothing ever remains the same. Joining the distinguished ranks of producers like Peter Rock, Q-Tip, DJ Premier, Large Professor, and L.E.S. propelled me to new heights of relevance and visibility within the hip-hop recording industry.

At the conclusion of my recording session with Nas, I returned to Rodney's home to continue collaborating on a few other tracks in his basement studio. While working with Rodney in Pleasantville for a second time, Raul introduced to me Marnet "Marni" Ali Williams. Marni is the older sister of Rozonda "Chilli" from the hit R&B group TLC. While meeting with Marni, I received a message from my managers sending me back to Los Angeles to begin working on a remix for the single "Red Light Special" from TLC's multiplatinum album *CrazySexyCool*. I was told the song was scheduled to have a video shot in two months, and the decision whether to use the remix or the original version produced by Babyface had not been made. If the label moved forward with the original production, there was a chance I would be considered for placement on the B-side (or "flip-side") of the single. Also known as a "bonus" track, B-sides were often given to new producers who showed potential in the recording industry. For instance, Run-DMC's "Peter Piper" was the B-side to the hit record "My Adidas" from the album *Raising Hell*.

## BLACK, YOUNG, AND HUNTED IN THE WIND

Leaving Pleasantville, I made my way to Jersey City to pick up traveling clothes and then to Philadelphia International Airport. I picked up my ticket at the check-in counter and proceeded to walk to my gate. I was two hours early, so I decided to eat at one of the adjoining restaurants before boarding. After finishing my meal, I returned to my gate and waited with the other travelers for our departure.

A middle-aged male tapped my shoulder. He flashed his badge: D.E.A. "Excuse me," he said. "Can you follow me into that room over there for a minute? I received a notification from the gate that there is something wrong with your ticket. I'm sure we can work this out rather quickly. Just come with me across the hall."

By then, other travelers at the gate were looking at me with suspicion. It was the same look I experienced while traveling to the 1995 Soul Train Music Awards. It was the look of the formulated opinion that I was guilty until proven innocent. There had to be something suspicious about a young Black male traveling by himself in first class on a premium flight from Philadelphia to Los Angeles on an early Friday evening. Something had to be wrong.

As we entered the room, two more D.E.A. agents requested my identification. As I turned over my driver's license, the other D.E.A. officer said, "Yeah, we've been watching you since you picked up your ticket. Why don't you have anything other than that knapsack on such a long flight?"

"Is it illegal for a Black man to carry a knapsack on a flight to Los Angeles?" I asked.

"Well, it depends on what you're carrying in that knapsack."

The third D.E.A. officer jumped into the discussion. "Would you mind if we take a look inside of your knapsack?"

I was exasperated. "Why? What do you think is in there?"

The officer responded, "Well, we see a lot of boys like you carrying drugs through this airport in knapsacks just like that."

"For your information," I told him, "I have two sets of clothes and a draft of a music contract. But if you think I have something else in the bag, take a look."

The three officers proceeded to huddle over my traveling bag. They slowly removed one item at a time. My Sony Walkman. Two pairs of Karl Kani jeans. Two Maurice Malone long-sleeve shirts. A pair of Penny Hardaway sneakers. Last, they removed a draft of the record contract submitted through Priority Records. The draft had been FedExed to my attention to initiate negotiations on my publishing rights for the song I recently completed with Nas.

After whispering among themselves for a little more than ten minutes, one agent said, "Well, I guess you really are somebody. Here's your bag. You're free to go."

"I didn't know I needed to be interrogated for it to be determined whether I'm worthy of your respect," I said, grabbing my belongings.

As I returned to my seat at the boarding gate, I couldn't help but notice I was the only person of color sitting at the gate. I was also the only person of color sitting in first class. Long before the increased rates of racial profiling of Muslims and Middle Easterners after September 11, 2001, people of color—young Black males especially—have been targeted under the suspicion of drug trafficking or other illegal activities.

King Downing, the national coordinator of the American Civil Liberties Union, was the victim of profiling by police in 2003 at Logan International Airport in Boston. Downing was stopped and questioned after arriving on a flight to attend a meeting on racial profiling. He sued the Massachusetts Port Authority, citing their violation of his constitutional rights.[4]

---

4. Michael Dwer/AP, "ACLU official alleges racial profiling at airport," MSNBC Travel News, December 3, 2007.

More recently, entertainers like Trae tha Truth, Migos, Gillie Da King, Eric André, and Clayton English have all given voice to their constitutional rights being violated through unreasonable searches, seizures, and racial discrimination. Data suggest drugs are rarely found during stops, and seized cash serves as a financial windfall for police departments. A large majority of Black rappers and comedians are paid in cash for their services. However, if they are unable to produce a receipt to validate their financial transactions, their cash is seized. Such artists are then inconvenienced with having to endure the legal process of reclaiming cash that had been unjustly confiscated by local police departments.

Comedian Eric André tweeted about his experience at the Atlanta airport in April 2021. André claimed he was racially profiled by two plain clothes Atlanta PD police officers while walking down to board his plane. The police claimed to be engaged in a "random" search for drugs and asked if they could search his body and possessions. In a scenario very similar to several I have also experienced while traveling as a young Black record producer, the police officers commenced with their search long after he passed security. André was the only person of color waiting in line.

When I was racially profiled in 1994, there was no data to track the frequency by which law enforcement officers interrogated people of color. However, police records from August 30, 2020, to April 30, 2021, show there were 402 jet bridge stops at the Atlanta airport. Of the 378 passengers whose race was listed, 211 people were Black (56 percent of those stopped) and 258 were people of color (68 percent of those stopped), André's lawsuit revealed. Out of the 402 total stops, only three reported drug seizures: 10 grams of drugs from one passenger, 26 grams of "suspected THC gummies" from a different passenger, and six prescription pills without a prescription from a third passenger, André's lawsuit read. Two of those people were charged. André's lawsuit also states that those 402 stops yielded more than $1 million in cash and money orders from twenty-five passengers, but only two people—the same caught with drugs—were charged. Eight people challenged their money seizures and Clayton County police settled each case, returning most of the money.[5]

After the five-and-a-half-hour flight from Philadelphia to Los Angeles, I deplaned and walked silently to the passenger pick-up section of LAX where Brett B. was waiting to bring me back to the studio Panorama City. For the next three days, I worked feverishly to create a remix for TLC's single. Needless to say, my submission did not stick; the executives at LaFace Records decided to move in a different direction. On a Thursday evening after my return, Brett B., Spyderman, and I drove over to Prince's new nightclub, Glam Slam. The club was enveloped with gold fabrics hanging from the walls and ceilings, purple dance floors, and Egyptian-style faces that peered down from the walls. Attending the club on this particular evening were the members of the group Club Nouveau. Snoop Dogg and staff members from Death Row Records stood alongside one of the far walls. The rapper Ice-T, DJ Ralph M, and an assortment of actors and performers like Jean-Claude Van Damme, Carmen Electra, Everlast, and the Lady of Rage mingled with one another, captivated by the creative aesthetic and hospitality of one of the greatest entertainers of all time. While reflecting upon my recent experience with Nas, I received another pager alert: "Def Jam is looking for remixes." I needed to pack up and head back to New York City within forty-eight hours.

---

5. "Comedians Eric André and Clayton English sue over Atlanta airport searches, *The Guardian*, October 12, 2022, https://www.theguardian.com/us-news/2022/oct/12/eric-andre-lawsuit-atlanta-airport-police-racial-profiling.

# 7

## MEETING THE SUFFERING
## WHERE THEY ARE

*And wherever he went, into villages or cities*
*or farms, they laid the sick in the marketplaces,*
*and begged him that they might touch*
*even the fringe of his cloak.*

**—Mark 6:56a**

When asked, "Who should be considered the greatest live musical entertainer of all time?" one would be hard pressed to find a list that does not include Michael Jackson, Elvis Presley, Beyoncé, Little Richard, James Brown, the Rolling Stones, Whitney Houston, Prince, Count Basie, or Aretha Franklin. When it comes to best live hip-hop performers, artists like Doug E. Fresh, LL Cool J, Run-DMC, Kendrick Lamar, DMX, Public Enemy, N.W.A., Queen Latifah, Naughty by Nature, Busta Rhymes, Big Daddy Kane, Missy Elliott, the Roots, and Grandmaster Flash and the Furious Five usually sit at the top of the list. Some might also include Eminem, Out-Kast, Luke Skywalker, 2 Live Crew, Onyx, Salt-N-Pepa, Three 6 Mafia, or Wu-Tang Clan. I was present in the summer of 1994 when Black

Moon, Wu-Tang Clan, Gang Starr, Queen Latifah, A Tribe Called Quest, SWV, and Arrested Development performed live at Hot 97 FM's "Summer Jam" rap concert. The inaugural concert took place at the Meadowlands Brendan Byrne Arena in East Rutherford, New Jersey.

In addition to all these entertainers, in my eyes Whodini has to be considered one of the greatest live performing groups of any genre or musical era. I experienced Whodini performing live for the very first time not too soon after recording the vocals to "My Mello My Man." Whodini was scheduled to perform at a live showcase in Atlanta during the summer of 1996. I was invited along with a group of others to accompany Whodini toward the stage where they would perform. As I walked toward the stage several yards behind Whodini, I noticed a commotion in front of the group. I couldn't see who was leading our entourage, but I noticed they were shouting vitriolic comments in the direction of a person in a room to our left. From the room, this person began spitting in the direction of those leading the entourage accompanying Whodini. As I passed the door, I was finally able to identify who was matching the vitriol of the group with his own. It was none other than Tupac.

## THE 1995 SOURCE AWARDS

In the summer of 1995, I was fully immersed in the work of producing additional songs for Perspective Records' recording artist Pudgee Tha Phat Bastard. The first two records, "Niguhz Fo Life" and "Dead Men Tell No Tales," were already completed; Pudgee and I were brainstorming possible creative directions for the remaining songs we intended to produce. While taking a break during one of our recording sessions at Platinum Island Studios, I received a message that tickets had been secured on my behalf for the upcoming Source Awards at the Paramount Theater at Madison Square Garden. The Source Awards was an awards ceremony created by the owners and creators of *The Source* hip-hop magazine, a rap periodical published semiannually about the latest trends circulating in the recording industry. New artists who submitted music projects to *The Source* received a review of one to five "mics" for the quality of their lyrical prowess and production. The Source Awards was developed as an extension of *The Source* brand. Since I produced two of the artists nominated for "New Artist of the Year" and "Lyricist of the Year" in Ill Al Skratch and Nas, respectively, it was recommended that I attend to show my support.

On the Source Awards platform, artists who were snubbed at the Grammy Awards could receive their recognition from an audience who felt that hip-hop was not adequately represented in the Grammy rap category. By the year 1990, hip-hop had evolved beyond the mainstream in which artists like Tone Loc, Will Smith, and Jazzy Jeff found a significant footing. The snubbing of artists and musical productions deemed by a large contingent of consumers to represent "real hip-hop" led to the creation of a full-scale award show where those artists who were considered "true to the game" could be properly acknowledged for their creative genius.

On August 3, hundreds of artists, record company executives, producers, and street promotion teams entered the Paramount Theater to see their favorite artists perform. Artists like Craig Mack, Faith Evans, Method Man, Dr. Dre, Snoop Dogg, Tha Dogg Pound, Bone Thugs-N-Harmony, DJ Quik, Da Brat, Junior M.A.F.I.A., and The Notorious B.I.G. took center stage, performing some of their most popular records for an ultrahyped crowd. Intermingled with the audience were the entourages who accompanied many artists to the show. The cameras broadcasting the live performances and award presentations could not capture the bottles of Jack Daniels, St. Ides beer, and reefer joints being passed back and forth from one row to the next. Nor could the cameras capture the tension that filled the room. By then, Death Row Records and Bad Boy Entertainment had reached a new level of competition and conflict. The tension in the air was not verbally communicated but was readily felt by those of us who attended.

The very first group of artists to perform at the Source Awards that night were Death Row Records' rappers: Tha Dogg Pound, Lady of Rage, Nate Dogg, Sam Sneed, DJ Quik, and Snoop Dogg. The theater was captivated by the sound quality of the West Coast style hip-hop tracks and the unique blend of lyrical performances offered by their artists. The set design for Death Row's artists was equally impactful. CEO Suge Knight spent over $100,000 to erect a prison tier in which all of Death Row's artists stood behind bars until they emerged individually to perform a snippet of their most current hit. Those of us who sat in the audience could not overlook the fact that in one of Death Row's staged prison cells was a cardboard cutout of Tupac. Tupac's cutout remained behind bars as if to suggest that he was now a member of Death Row but had not received his release date just yet. Those of us who were in the know were aware Tupac was still serving time at the Clinton Correctional Facility in Dannemora, New York. Showcasing Tupac's image behind bars on a Death Row set sent a clear message to the East Coast artists and record executives that a formidable partnership was emerging right before their very eyes.

Hip-hop historians and cultural content curators have often suggested that the 1995 Source Awards is most remembered for Death Row CEO Suge Knight's sneak diss against Bad Boy Entertainment CEO P-Diddy. After ascending the stage to receive the award for "Movie Soundtrack of the Year," Suge Knight mocked P-Diddy by stating belligerently: "Any artist out there that wants to be an artist or stay a star—and don't want to worry about an executive producer trying to be all in the videos, all on the records, dancing—come to Death Row!" Other hip-hop historians recount the moment when Atlanta's rap group OutKast won the award for "Best New Rap Group." In response to the boos and jeers coming from a predominantly New York audience, André 3000 famously shouted into the microphone, "The South has something to say!"

For those of us deeply entrenched in the inner workings of the hip-hop industry, nothing was more pivotal at the 1995 Source Awards than the symbolism portrayed in Death Row's stage set. People sitting next to me and behind me began to whisper that Tupac was negotiating a new deal and intended to perform under the Death Row banner once he was freed from incarceration. Little did any of us know that Tupac and Suge

Knight were already privately negotiating Tupac's release from prison. Tupac was close to signing a three-album record deal worth $3.5 million. In early October of 1995, Tupac signed his new deal with Death Row Records and was subsequently released from Clinton Correctional Facility on a $1.4 million bail package. Just eleven months after being assaulted at Quad Studios on November 30, 1994, Tupac was released from prison pending an appeal of his conviction for sexual assault. Much had changed since that cold night in November 1994. Now, in the summer of 1996, I crossed Tupac's orbit again. This time, he was spitting at an entourage he felt threatened by.

## WHEN JESUS MET THE SUFFERING

Wherever Jesus set his foot in Gennesaret, the sick and poor clamored for his attention. Unlike the other healing stories in Mark's Gospel, this one contains no teaching of Jesus, no dialogue with the demon possessed or the afflicted. Whoever Jesus touched, and whoever touched Jesus, was healed. The compassion of Jesus fed, satisfied, and healed the crowds who gathered to be set free from their afflictions.

Yet Mark leaves a larger question unresolved: Would those who experienced Jesus's healing power take the next step in entering further into fellowship with him? The physical blessings of Jesus were not intended to be an end in and of themselves. To the contrary, the blessings of Jesus presented a fork in the road, offering an alternative path toward a deeper understanding of God's character and Jesus's mission on Earth. Mark's Gospel consistently presents examples of Jesus's unrelenting goodness being shared with the disrupted. In the story of the disciples trapped in the middle of the Sea of Galilee, Jesus even used a storm as a catalyst to meet the needs of a people who were sick, poor, and powerless.

The church (re)learned during the pandemic that the only way to effectively address the needs of those who suffer is to meet people where they are. In the absence of in-person worship during quarantine, many churches across the globe turned to a varying assortment of technological tools to foster community with those who were displaced and disconnected by the pandemic. Human beings genuinely love authentic connection and desire to belong. Many of the restrictions to belonging imposed by congregations—proper attire or social class, certain jewelry or ways of speaking—were suddenly irrelevant in the context of lives-treaming worship services. It's a lesson the church can learn from hip-hop, too, that what an individual wears or where they work can never be the more predominant concern over an individual's right to be treated as a child of God. To touch, whether it be in person or online, is to love.

March 15, 2020, marked the very first Sunday when First Baptist Church of Hillside transitioned toward becoming a completely virtual ministry. The New Jersey and New York region was considered the epicenter of the pandemic, with reports of COVID-19 cases increasing by the day, and quarantine restrictions were implemented rapidly. On March 9, Governor Phil Murphy declared a state of emergency. On March 10, Rutgers University announced classes had been canceled, and it eventually moved all instruction online. On March 11, Princeton University ordered all its students to leave campus and stay at home. On March 12, New Jersey Governor Murphy announced the cancellation of all public meetings that exceeded 250 people. By March 15, thirty-one new coronavirus cases were reported, bringing the total number of deaths to ninety-eight. By March 31, the total number of coronavirus deaths surged to 267, with at least 18,696 total coronavirus cases being reported statewide. Curfews from 10:00 P.M. to 6:00 A.M. were imposed in practically every municipality throughout the state. Public schools were closed, restaurants began to shut down, and Newark International Airport began to suspend services to regional and international airlines.

The spiritual officers and support staff at First Baptist Church of Hillside began to wrestle with what it meant to be the church in the middle of a pandemic. If the church is fundamentally composed of preaching, teaching, worshiping, serving, witnessing, and fostering a sense of belonging, how would it function in the context of a pandemic? I insisted in our strategic leadership meetings that not even a pandemic should be able to stop a church from functioning as "the church." Very passionately, I emphasized that the church is made up of people with varying spiritual gifts and resources. I believe members of the *ecclesia* (literally, "called-out ones") have the skills and ingenuity needed to reimagine what it means to be in community—no matter how disruptive an unexpected storm may be. Such clarity of mission and purpose was and still is directly tied to a fundamental belief that Jesus can use such storms to reach the suffering, displaced, and disheartened.

Across its digital platforms, our church preached the mountaintops and valleys of faith, the hopes and the tests that fill life with unpredictable moments. Virtual sermons conveyed the notion that, while suffering is inevitable, the cross serves as our spiritual GPS and as a reminder that we are in relationship with a Savior who is well acquainted with suffering. As real as the cross was for Jesus, God's redemptive power at the resurrection was even more profound, and, because of the resurrection, we now have a relationship with a Savior who yields power over our every wilderness season and valley experience. Moreover, through faith in Jesus Christ, we have access to resurrection power that enables us to not only endure suffering but create a new life in the midst a storm. Online midweek and weekend teaching series were broadcast to revisit the basic tenets of the Christian faith so that our shared discipleship was nourished and strengthened. Sound theological teaching through the pandemic's radical disruption helped parishioners articulate faith in a God who is present and actively working through historical events to reach a determined end.

Our all-virtual platforms allowed the church to respond to God's call to worship in ways that fostered engagement with each other and with those who streamed from places as far as Canada, Jamaica, Ghana, England, and Australia. For the first time ever, First Baptist Church of Hillside functioned as an international ministry hub through which Christians from separate continents could respond to God's invitation to gather simultaneously. A new virtual-only ministry called Virtual Ambassadors for Christ was created to engage online worshipers during the service and foster a sense of belonging. Worship became a more visually engaging experience as graphics were used to offer visual imagery. Now worshipers were not only hearing the word and praying the word, they were "seeing" the word as well. Every invitation to discipleship, to join our e-church, or to receive prayer at the conclusion of online worship was communicated audibly, visually, and artistically. The pandemic opened a door for the church to create an authentic, multisensory worship experience that I believe allowed for a more meaningful encounter with God.

In addition to expanding our virtual presence, the pandemic offered an opportunity for the members of First Baptist Church of Hillside to expand our community presence beyond the local municipality and county. Partnerships with businesses and nonprofits enabled the church to serve constituents who traveled from as far as Connecticut and Philadelphia to receive free vaccinations and health screenings. The church partnered with local government to provide rental assistance for those who lost jobs due to COVID-19-related downsizing. Multiple back-to-school outreach initiatives, school tutoring opportunities, and weekly community-wide food distribution programs served as examples in which the church reimagined the various ways it could engage a community radically disrupted by the pandemic.

Meeting the people where they are, as Jesus did in Gennesaret, requires a working theology that understands God's desire to dwell among the afflicted. In fact, God prefers to dwell among those who are in great need and whose lives have been disrupted by life's storms. In a world gripped with fear, hatred, and distrust, it is imperative that church engages in the continuous work of reimagining what it means to be a part of a called community sent out to minister to (Matthew 28:19–20). Worshiping, teaching, witnessing, serving, and discipling require new ministry models that fit our present context. If the unchurched and nonreligious demographic in America continues to rise, as suggested Peter Smith in his insightful article "America's Nonreligious Are a Growing, Diverse Phenomenon: They Really Don't Like Religion," the church will have no choice but to rethink its methods of engagement if it intends to reach those who have never attended a church.[1] We look to the model of Jesus, who was as fully engaged in the work of prayer as he was in the work of calming the storm or in the work of healing the masses.

## WHEN THE CHURCH MET THE SUFFERING IN FLINT

When the church is at its best, it pools its resources to meet the needy wherever they are. This is a work of justice, and the work of justice is centered upon what the scriptures deem righteous in the eyes of God rather than what the world thinks is best for its own utilitarian good. To do justice is to take action and confront evil, to care for the vulnerable, and to make right that which in society sin has made wrong. It is ongoing work. The psalmist reminds the observant reader, "Give justice to the weak and the orphan; maintain the right of the lowly and the destitute" (Psalm 82:3).

In April 2014, the emergency managers of Flint, Michigan, approved an executive decision to draw water from the Flint River rather than purchasing water from Lake Huron via Detroit, in an effort to save the city money. Unfortunately, the city of Flint's water filtration plant was ill-equipped to properly treat the warmer river water, resulting in lead-contaminated water streaming through the city's pipes. Residents, of whom more than 52 percent are Black, immediately began to complain of the water's stench—an olfactory alarm that something was terribly wrong with their drinking water system. What residents could not see was that the untreated, highly corrosive river water caused lead from the aging pipes to leach into the city's water supply. Citizens of Flint began to suffer severe rashes and hair loss. By early 2015, local doctors in Flint were reporting high levels of toxins in blood samples in the city's children. City officials declared a state of emergency and switched the water supply back to Detroit water, but not before compromising the health of the city's children.

---

1. Peter Smith, "America's Nonreligious Are a Growing, Diverse Phenomenon: They Really Don't Like Religion," AP News, October 5, 2023, https://apnews.com/article/nonreligious-united-states-nones-spirituality-humanist-91bb8430280c88fd88530a7ad64b03f8.

In response, the church pooled its resources in a joint effort to help provide water to the more than fifty thousand households in Flint who had no access to clean water for longer than a year. Michigan Conference of the United Church of Christ and the Michigan Region of the Christian Church (Disciples of Christ) launched "The Gospel in Action—Flint."[2] Thousands of faith communities like New Birth Missionary Baptist Church in Atlanta, Hartford Memorial Baptist Church in Detroit, the Greater Allen A.M.E. Cathedral of New York, Catholic Charities, the Flint Jewish Federation, Mississippi Boulevard Christian Church, and the Michigan Muslim Community Council worked with agencies, mission-based conventions, and organizations to distribute tons of bottled water to the constituents of Flint. Social justice advocates, grassroots organizations, and legal think-tanks joined in supporting the efforts of legal experts to challenge the reckless decisions made by city officials and press charges against those whose actions could be proven to be criminal in court. In early 2016, a coalition of citizens and advocacy groups—including Flint resident Melissa Mays, the local group Concerned Pastors for Social Action, NRDC, and the ACLU of Michigan—sued city and state officials to secure safe drinking water for Flint residents. Among the demands of the suit: the proper testing and treatment of water for lead and the replacement of all the city's lead pipes. In March 2016, the coalition took additional legal action to address another litany of urgent needs, filing a motion to ensure that all residents—including children, the elderly, and others unable to reach the city's free water distribution centers—would have free access to safe drinking water through a bottled water delivery service, a robust filter installation, and a maintenance program.[3]

The collective efforts of these advocacy groups and grassroots organizations eventually paid off. In November 2016, a federal judge sided with

2. Carol Fouke-Mpoyo, "UCC, Disciples Partner to Bring Water, Justice to Flint, Mich.," United Church of Christ, January 20, 2016, https://www.ucc.org/disaster_flint_water_update/.

3. Melissa Denchak, "Flint Water Crisis: Everything You Need to Know," NRDC, April 16, 2024, https://www.nrdc.org/stories/flint-water-crisis-everything-you-need-know#summary.

Flint residents and ordered the implementation of door-to-door delivery of bottled water to every home without a properly installed and maintained faucet filter. A more momentous win came the following March with a major settlement requiring the city to replace the city's thousands of lead pipes with funding from the state. Further funding for comprehensive tap water testing was guaranteed, as well as a faucet filter installation and education program, free bottled water through the following summer, and continued health programs to help residents deal with the residual effects of Flint's tainted water.[4] While more work is to be done to secure justice, equity, and economic reparations in the city of Flint, the mobilization of the church in support of Flint residents is a reminder to the postquarantine church that taking action for justice is essential to our Christian love ethic. When the church sees itself as an equal partner in a justice-seeking community, it will not fear pooling its resources to meet the downtrodden and oppressed wherever they are and offering the ministry of healing to those who have been disrupted by the winds of injustice.

## THE ECHOES IN THE WIND

On July 5, 1994, Tupac was captured on camera spitting at reporters and cameramen as he exited the New York State Supreme Court in downtown Manhattan. Almost three decades later, in the 2023 docuseries about Tupac and his mother, entitled *Dear Mama*, Tupac's Aunt Glo reviews old video footage of the spitting incident.[5] Watching the footage, Aunt Glo suggests that Tupac may have spat at the reporters because he was afraid for his life—threatened by the extremely biased media coverage that portrayed him as an unbridled beast of passion, the mounting legal troubles taxing his career as a superstar recording artist and promising actor, and the potential for a violent encounter with the street figures. Spitting, in Aunt Glo's opinion, was a nervous response to a hostile environment.

---

4. Ibid.

5. Allen Hughes, *Dear Mama*, Paramount Pictures, 2023, https://www.imdb.com/title/tt6871344/.

Up until I heard Aunt Glo's reflection captured in Allen Hughes' groundbreaking docuseries, I could not make sense of Tupac spitting at the entourage that led Whodini and I onto the stage at that showcase in the summer of 1996. It finally dawned on me that Tupac felt threatened by certain individuals who were not official members of Whodini's entourage; these individuals only appeared to be so. They never joined us on the stage, nor did they leave the venue with us once Whodini completed their set. With the exception of Whodini, Tupac could not distinguish the rest of us from anyone affiliated with the goons who assaulted him at Quad Studios on that fateful night on November 30, 1994. The image of Tupac looking at us from head to toe as we walked to the stage remains fresh in my mind. Clearly, he was making a quick assessment as to whether we were friend or foe. The security who accompanied Tupac in that room had one hand on his shoulder and the other hand on their hip.

. Acoustical consultants say that wind from a powerful storm can bend sound waves and, by forming walls that propel sound back and forth at the rate of the wind propulsion, capture echoes. Depending upon the strength of the walls within the wind, sound can travel great distances without any degradation in amplitude modulation. Both the source of the wind and the character of the object(s) captured within its path determine the nature of the sound being echoed and the duration of its amplification.

I believe we all walk according to the speed and pace of the winds that greet us at birth. Our life's journey is greatly influenced by the echoes of the pains and tribulations of our past. Depending upon the intensity of the winds, our life can be trapped in invisible walls that hinder our ability to hear anything other than the repeated echoes we inherited at birth. For some of us, those echoes are riddled with harmful messages of doubt, fear, abandonment, and abuse. Until those winds are disrupted by a counter-wind, our echoes remain the same. The repetition of acute trauma and systemic oppression can paralyze us to the degree that we cannot imagine ourselves outside of the walls formed by the stormy winds engulfing us. When Tupac spat into the wind, I envision echoes from a troubled past that failed to capture the true nature of Tupac's intellectual genius. Without the radical disruption of a counter-wind, it seems logical why Tupac struggled to break free from the echoes reflecting the existential agonies he had suffered since he was a child.

It could be argued, just as I believe was the case with Tupac, that people walk into our churches carrying the echoes in the wind tunnels of their own painful past. Unless radically disrupted, many remain paralyzed by repetitive messages suggesting they will continue to live life in agony without the promise of future hope. The church of today needs a working theology that allows for the belief in a disruptive God if we are to be effective in our call to reach those in the boat and those in Gennesaret. The Apostle Paul speaks of the Holy Spirit in Romans 8:1–2 as a counter-wind to his lamentable echoes in Romans 7. Jesus, too, reminds us that God breaks into our echoes with counter-winds that change our life's trajectory. In the case of the disciples who struggled at sea, Jesus broke into the wind and compelled it to become silent. In doing so, Jesus also broke open the walls within the storm echoing the doubts and fears of the disciples.

Making sense of the echoes requires the church to have a compassionate heart toward those whom Jesus identified in Matthew 25:45 as "the least of these": those among us who hunger or thirst, as well as those who are naked, homeless, sick, incarcerated, systematically oppressed, and those who are denied access to the righteousness of God. They are both unemployed and underemployed; they are without health care or advocacy. "The least of these" lack political representation and, in many instances, are led by derelict politicians who have been seduced by corporate interests. They are youth who are being abused at home, and children who are underserved and underfunded in their public schools. "The least of these" often consist of those who suffer from drug addiction, mental illness, a criminal past, broken families, sexual abuse, and parental abandonment.

From the Gospel of Matthew's perspective, "the least of these" are to be respected and served as much as the king on the throne. In the eyes of God, it does not matter if those being served are disciples or not. Jesus used the radical disruption of a storm as an opportunity to redirect the disciples to a region they had not planned to go. In the boat, Jesus silenced their internal echoes of defeat with his presence and then offered a counter-wind of hope, which became a mechanism for service. Just as Jesus did on the Sea of Galilee, the church can use the disruptive winds of the pandemic as an opportunity to journey into spaces otherwise deemed unreachable. New platforms and new methods of ministry have afforded the church an opportunity to break through the walls of those who still feel paralyzed by fear and to silence the echoes of their despair that reverberate at the thought of reentering into their church home, job, or society in general. Constructing a working theology of holy disruption makes room for new ways to meet people where they are. It also enabled First Baptist Church of Hillside to create virtual platforms and cyber-ministries and digital town talks that allowed participants to "touch" the hem of Jesus's garment. We still render these pastoral care offerings today. These virtual points of contact continue to help those who struggle to hear a different voice beyond the echoes that trap people in the winds of fear and resignation.

**TAKING THE STAGE**

I took my place in the rear of the stage with the other members of our entourage while Whodini grabbed their microphones and made their way to the front. For the next twenty minutes, Whodini performed effortlessly with perfect cadence and a call and response comparable to any Black Baptist church in the South. With one hit after the next, Ecstasy and Jahlil led the audience through a series of urban anthems that brought to our remembrance the days of silk BVD t-shirts, Lee pinstripe jeans, suede Puma sneakers with fat laces, and beaver Kangol hats. Grandmaster Dee set the stage on fire with "Five Minutes of Funk," followed by "The Freaks Come Out at Night." As the crowd continued to ascend in its fervor, Whodini transitioned into two other hip-hop classics: "Big Mouth" and "Funky Beat." Then Ecstasy recited the opening lyrics to "Friends," a song

Nas recently sampled to create his own hit with Fugees rapper Lauryn Hill, entitled "If I Ruled the World." With each throb of the bassline, each crash of the kick and snare, the entire room lost itself in euphoria. Grandmaster Dee switched back and forth between "Friends" and "If I Ruled the World" as the crowd followed along lyric for lyric.

Marveling at the genius performance of Whodini, I looked to my right to see if Tupac had settled down after having been so intensely inflamed at the beginning of the showcase. From my vantage point on the stage, I could not see if his room was still occupied. It wasn't until I exited the stage with Whodini that I realized that the room was now empty. What remained were chairs piled into a stack at the front entrance closest to the stage. The rear of the room was left in disarray. It was as if a turbulent wind had torn Tupac out of the room as quickly as he appeared. My pager buzzed. This time I was summoned to take a meeting in Jersey City with one of my favorite rappers of all time.

# 8

# A GOD OF NEW BEGINNINGS

*[A]nd all who touched it were healed.*

**—Mark 6:56b**

Living in Los Angeles as an accomplished music producer affords an individual the opportunity to meet some of the kindest and most gifted people. It became a common occurrence to receive surprise visits from artists like Uptown Records' hip-hop group Lost Boyz in the early afternoon and then host a party welcoming actors like Tyrese Gibson, Bokeem Woodbine, and Trichina Arnold in the evening. Arguably the most beautiful soul I ever encountered in the entertainment industry was Tommy "Tiny" Lister, Jr. Tommy Lister is famously known for playing the bodacious South Central Los Angeles character "Deebo" in the urban classic film *Friday*, directed by F. Gary Gray and written by O'Shea "Ice Cube" Jackson, Sr.

I met Tommy Lister on the set of the video shoot for the lead single I produced with Shaquille O'Neal, "You Can't Stop the Reign." This was the second version of the original music composition featuring The Notorious B.I.G.; the original version was entitled "Still Can't Stop the Reign." In the video, Tommy Lister played the role of Shaq's archenemy who joins forces with the devious character Enrico Gates and deploys usurpers to undermine Shaq's attempt to create a new mafioso-styled musical conglomerate called T.W.Is.M. The video escalates to a battle between Shaq, Tommy, and Enrico Gates in which Shaq defeats his enemies and successfully unites T.W.Is.M. When I first met Tommy, I assumed his personality would match the personality of Deebo. I was anticipating a gregarious, chauvinistic individual who imposed his will on others without apology.

To the contrary, Tommy's very first words to me were, "Will you pray for me?" When I told him I didn't quite know how to pray, he responded, "Well, let me pray for you," and then proceeded to offer a short prayer for my well-being, peace of mind, and protection in the music industry.

I made mention of the fact that Rodney and the Jerkins family, along with Clean Cut, were the very first to model what it could possibly look like to be Christian and formidable contributors to the recording indus- try. Tommy was the very first actor to model what it was like to be both Christian and a professional actor in the entertainment industry. There are some who argue that a Christian is forced to compromise their faith if they aspire to be successful in the world of entertainment, or that they will be tempted by the industry to compromise their moral compass and faith system. I can only testify that—through the likes of Rodney, Clean Cut, and Tommy—God was actively engaged in the work of sending consecutive disruptive moments that ultimately led to my radical encounter with Jesus Christ in the early winter of 1996. I have argued throughout the writing of this book that God uses historic events, moments of personal and collective crisis, and many people to alter our life's trajectory. While we may experience these cataclysmic moments as unexpected storms, the storms are sacred because God is actively working at the center of them. While at the center, God assures us that we are not alone. God is working on a plan, and God's plan is always for our good. Moreover, there is life on the other side of our sacred storms. We are invited to hold on to God's unchanging hand until our storms subside.

## A DISRUPTED PLAN

At the conclusion of the video shoot in Los Angeles with Shaq, discussion began about a road trip to attend the Mike Tyson versus Bruce Seldon fight at the MGM Grand Garden Arena in Las Vegas. Billed as "Liberation" by promoters, this fight was Mike Tyson's third since his release from prison. Tyson had paid $4 million for the WBC's number one contender, Lennox Lewis, to step aside, thus allowing Tyson to face Seldon for the WBA Heavyweight title on September 7, 1996. The group of us still in Los Angeles after the video shoot began to make plans to attend the Tyson fight. That is, except me. Tommy Lister's prayers for protection and direction kept echoing in my subconsciousness. I couldn't muster up the will to book a room at the MGM to watch the fight with my colleagues. When asked if I was planning to attend, I said I wasn't sure. In reality, I was very sure. Something about going to Las Vegas did not sit well with me. Instead, I booked a flight back to New Jersey. God had a different plan in mind.

Upon arriving in New Jersey in late August 1996, I accepted an invitation to a sit-down meeting with the management division of Queen Latifah's Flavor Unit Entertainment. Flavor Unit Entertainment managed distinguished recording artists and music producers, as well as producing movie soundtracks, films, and television shows. Shirley Bell asked me to consider being managed by Flavor Unit Management exclusively. At the time, Flavor Unit Management was already managing Queen Latifah, Apache, Naughty By Nature, OutKast, and Bryce Wilson from Groove Theory. Shirley impressed upon me that, with Flavor Unit and Queen Latifah's support, I could ascend to even greater heights—not just as a music producer, but also as an entrepreneur. I pondered the pitch as Shirley walked me around Flavor Unit Headquarters—a converted historic firehouse in downtown Jersey City—introducing me to the administrative staff on hand. I found Queen Latifah's mother, Mrs. Rita Owens, to be the most gracious woman I have ever met. Mrs. Owens was the light and joy that made Flavor Unit headquarters illuminate as if the glory of God were in each room she inhabited. She made me feel like I was a part of the Owens family. The entire staff at Flavor Unit was gracious and kind. Although my stay with Flavor Unit Management would be brief, the time I spent with the entire Flavor Unit establishment remained (and remains to this very day) meaningful to me.

At the conclusion of my meeting with Shirley Bell, she offered to pray for my discernment concerning this opportunity. After she prayed, I asked, "Do you feel a wind blowing in here?"

"I don't feel anything at all," she responded.

I left the firehouse pondering my final decision.

## IT ONLY TAKES ONE TOUCH

For the Gospel of Mark, faith was the catalyst by which the masses came to Jesus for healing, trusting Jesus to be a priestly figure. Many believed if they could simply touch the fringe of Jesus's cloak, they would be miraculously healed (Mark 6:56b; also Mark 3:10 and 5:28). The healing miracles in Gennesaret were contingent upon those who were sick being able to get close to Jesus. Jesus needed to be seen and then accessed.

Having pastored at First Baptist Church of Hillside for longer than fifteen years, I have witnessed the power of healing transmitted through the gift of touch. I have seen a woman on the verge of death with leukemia miraculously recover into full remission through the power of touch. I have witnessed individuals approach the altar with a walking cane on a Sunday morning and suddenly return to their seat, never to pick up their cane again. I have observed people who suffered chronic headaches and were diagnosed with a brain tumor miraculously report that their tumor disappeared all because of a touch in the sanctuary. I have seen worshipers who come to church hunched over with debilitating arthritis declare that the pain miraculously went away after receiving a touch. These people came to church trapped in their own personal storm. For some, the storms were physical. For others, the storms were spiritual or psychological. The one thing they all shared was the belief that their storms would subside and they could live life anew if they received a touch from Jesus. For these people, like those in the region of Gennesaret, faith in a living God who has power to heal can lead to a life of new beginnings.

What, then, shall we say about the healing touch in this post-quarantine era of platforms and virtual ministry? I would say opportunities still abound if we believe that the afflicted can be healed through touch. A touch from Jesus can be received beyond the traditional methods of laying on hands or touching the minister's robe. We touch people through transformational preaching whether in-person or online. We touch people through impactful teaching in the sanctuary, through a podcast, or with a prerecorded lesson posted on YouTube. We touch people through prayers conveyed from the pulpit and through mass text messages. We touch people through acts of kindness that model what it means to love one's neighbor in the way God loves us.

We also touch people when we show up outside the walls of the church and meet people at their point of need. The masses in Gennesaret were healed because Jesus was accessible to them. The hem of Jesus's garment can only have impact if both it and him are allowed to be seen. During the pandemic, the S.I.S. Ministry of First Baptist Church of Hillside made a commitment to feed every mother within the township who felt underappreciated or struggled with pandemic-related unemployment. Rather than insist that mothers in Hillside come to the church, the S.I.S. Ministry partnered with a local restaurant to prepare free three-course dinners. By the end of the day, a number of mothers received free dinners, gift cards, and prayer as a courtesy from the S.I.S. Ministry. Testimonies continue to pour in from those who were impacted by a group of volunteers who chose to partner with God and make Jesus accessible to those in need.

We touch people when we host expungement clinics that help the poor and ex-convicts secure better jobs. Individuals are often prevented from gaining employment or a promotion because of prior criminal offenses that have not been expunged from their records. When churches partner with local police departments, county officials, and legal aides to support "second chance" workers through the expungement process, whole families and communities can receive a healing touch. Through New Hope Baptist Church of Elizabeth and First Baptist Church of Hillside's partnership with the National Action Network (NAN) and the prosecutor of Union County, I have witnessed individuals who were recently released from prison enter an expungement clinic in tears. Out on work release, these individuals automatically assume that the list of charges and convictions will never be removed from their rap sheet. Through the collaboration of churches, nonprofits, grassroots organizations, and civic leaders, these at-risk individuals are able to pare down their criminal history. In some instances, their records are expunged altogether, leading to shouts and uncontrollable wails of joy at the legal aid table. I have seen a sixty-four-year-old man cry for joy because twenty years of criminal history was immediately expunged. You cannot tell me this was not a touch from Jesus; this man was healed of multiple afflictions.

We touch people when we form relationships with local municipalities, county agencies, and nonprofits like United Way, YMCA, and YWCA through which we offer financial relief for those who cannot keep up with rent, mortgage, or utilities. In Black communities especially, families are still digging their way out of debt accrued during the pandemic. Without alternative sources of financial assistance, poverty can become an echoing storm, splitting apart our homes and destroying the morale of parents. We touch people when we provide mental health services for children and youth who are considering suicide because of bullying or overexposure to violence. Through social media, our youth are being overwhelmed with a culture of perfectionism projecting the notion that mistakes are impermissible and one's identity is solely wrapped up in winning. Through fragmentation in the home, our youth are experiencing increased anxiety and a general sense of hopelessness. However, I have also witnessed children, youth, and their families experience the redemptive love of God through mental health care services provided by churches, counselors, and social workers partnered with trauma therapists, psychiatrists, and mental health centers. Our children and youth can experience a touch from God when we work together in our communities to secure resources for the care that our people need.

With a touch, and in most instances multiple touches, storms that echo relentlessly in the lives of the needy and the afflicted can be interrupted. A crosswind can come when the hem of Jesus—his love embodied in tangible acts of love and justice—is made accessible. When the church takes the initiative to make Jesus accessible, both in the sanctuary, online, and in the community, the noise of uncertainty and doubt is diminished, and new beginnings can be envisioned by those in search of hope.

## BITTER WATER INTO SWEET

The Bible offers a multitude of examples in which God used individuals to heal others through the ministry of touch—and not only the touch of a hand, but at times, the touch of instruments used by individuals who firmly believed in the healing power of God. Exodus 15:22–25 records the story of Moses and the ancient Israelites who, having crossed the Red Sea, enter a vast, rugged, and sparsely populated wilderness region identified as Shur. The route Moses followed through Shur offered an easier passage on foot for travelers, so long as they brought ample water supplies with them until they reached the next watering hole. It is reasonable to assume the people carried water with them in skins for both themselves and their livestock to consume. Most likely they had enough water to survive in their sojourn until they reached the water at Marah. Unfortunately, the water there was bitter (Exodus 15:23). While not at the point of delirium, the Israelites were overcome with panic and assumed that, having exhausted their water supply, they would die from thirst in the middle of the wilderness.

The author of this sacred text wants to convey to readers that the crisis at Marah was a test of faith for the ancient Israelites. They asked, "What shall we drink?" (Exodus 15:24). To pose the question was not sinful; however, their attitude and forgetfulness of God's power in a moment crisis could be deemed sinful. Their God Yahweh had just split the Red Sea in two on their behalf. It was Yahweh who led them by a pillar of cloud in the day and fire at night. Rather than remembering the Lord's faithfulness and seeking an answer from the God who led them, the people turned to Moses with their complaint. As in other events along the Israelites' journey toward Canaan, the people complained when they did not have what they expected. No matter the extent of God's miracles, when crises arose the Israelites often failed to trust that God would meet their needs. Since the Garden of Eden, disobedience ensues when trust falters; once disobedience takes root, sin abounds.

Moses turned to Yahweh, and in doing so, Moses participated in a supernatural demonstration of God's presence and provision. God showed Moses a piece of wood and instructed him to throw it into the bitter water. The power of healing touch was conveyed through wood touching water. God can heal in ways that may not include bodily contact—a point that should resonate with the postquarantine church striving to reach individuals and communities by alternative means. Moses did not touch the water, but the stick he had touched caused what had been bitter to change into something now sweet. Because of Moses's faith and obedience to God, God's care was demonstrated and the Israelites were replenished.

Is there a way to reimagine the impact the church can make by reviewing what God has placed in our hands? Moses had a stick. What do we have? When I think about the blessed soul of a former member, Mrs. Corliss Saney, who served as an usher and took pride in placing a church bulletin into a member's hand with delicate care, I am reminded that God can change someone's bitter week into something sweet through one simple interaction. What Mrs. Saney accomplished through the touch of a Sunday bulletin is no less important than the touches provided by our Virtual Ambassadors Ministry when engaging our online worshipers. Whether in person or online, the church cannot be afraid to rethink the power of touch. Through technological resources that have been consecrated to God, the church can be just as effective in healing through touch as it was prior to the onset of the pandemic. Our touch can embody the compassion and healing power of a God who turned the bitter waters of Marah into a source of sweet replenishment—the same power that through Jesus healed the afflicted in Gennesaret so that they could be restored and by faith be made whole.

## WHEN THE MIGHTY FALL

Two days after sitting in the Flavor Unit Entertainment office in Jersey City, I received a call from Shirley Bell, asking if I would be interested in remixing a single from SWV's second album, *New Beginning*. In the early 1990s, SWV (Sisters with Voices) was a favorite R&B group. Hits like "Weak," "Right Here," "I'm So into You," and "You're the One" became national anthems to a young hip-hop generation just beginning to mature in its self-identity and capacity to manage romantic relationships. The most appealing traits of SWV were their diverse vocal ability and unique set of individual personalities. Cheryl "Coko" Gamble was distinctly different from Tamara "Taj" George, and Taj was distinctly different from Leanne "Lelee" Lyons. A hybrid mix of gospel, R&B, and hip-hop, SWV proved themselves as one of the best-selling female groups in the recording industry in the mid-1990s.

Once again, I returned to Chung King Studios on the twelfth floor of 170 Varick Street in Hudson Square. I invited Clean Cut and David Caton to assist me in creating a sound that would amplify their vocal performance on the single "It's All About U." I also requested the services of the amazing sound engineer Dexter Simmons, whom I had met through Rodney Jerkins. Dexter had already mixed music compositions for OutKast, Gina Thompson, S.H.E., Whodini, and Head Nod on the *Panther* movie soundtrack, and he later mixed hits for Brandy, Monifah, Monica, Backstreet Boys, and Whitney Houston. I intended to use the percussion sounds from the rapper Special Ed's hit single "I Got It Made," and there was simply no better engineer than Dexter who possessed the skill to bring out the punch and snap from the kick and snare in the Special Ed drum sample.

Within twelve hours, the remix was properly synced to the two-inch tape. Clean Cut added a powerful rap just behind the second bridge, and

David Caton added a genius chord arrangement. By the end of the recording session, I entered into a handshake agreement with Dexter's manager for Dexter to mix all of my music productions moving forward. Dexter had an amazing ability to amplify any percussion sound into a thick frequency that made a producer's drum "slap." By September 5, I turned over the DAT recording of the session to Shirley at Flavor Unit Entertainment, who informed me that megaproducer Allstar had also completed his own version of the same remix. Allstar was famously known for having produced SWV's platinum single "Anything" featuring Wu-Tang for the *Above the Rim* movie soundtrack in 1993. There was a strong likelihood that either RCA Records or the group SWV would choose Allstar's remix before ever hearing my version.

On September 6, I received several calls from colleagues asking if I would reconsider flying out to Las Vegas for the Mike Tyson fight. I strongly reconsidered my initial refusal. There was no point in sitting at home, waiting for RCA Records to make a decision. I could preoccupy my creative thoughts with a change of scenery. Taking a red-eye flight to Las Vegas that evening would have placed me in Las Vegas by 5:00 A.M. the following morning, Saturday. Despite the hard consideration, I elected not to go to Las Vegas. I couldn't explain why, but I simply decided it would be best for me to remain in New Jersey. Around 3:00 A.M. on Sunday, September 8, Tupac Shukar was fatally shot on the corner of East Flamingo Road and Koval Lane in Las Vegas.

In his contribution to Anthony Pinn's *Religion in Hip Hop: Mapping the New Terrain in the US*, Daniel White-Hodge notes that Tupac's death marked the beginning of what he describes as a "Ghetto Saints Era."[1] For many, Tupac was a transcendent force who gave voice to the frustrations, fears, and worries of a youth culture that felt as though it had no advocate to call its own. To this massive group of listeners, Tupac

---

1. "Methods for the Prophetic: Tupac Shakur, Lauryn Hill, and the Case for Ethnolifehistory," 24–37, in Anthony Pinn, *Religion in Hip Hop: Mapping the New Terrain in the US*, edited by Monica R. Miller and Bernard "Bun B" Freeman (New York: Bloomsbury Academic, 2015).

embodied both the best and the most conflicted aspirations of a generation seeking a path forward in a world governed by systems that shunned the artistic expressions of the Black body. Tupac, possessing a postrevolutionary spirit, bridged the descendants of the Black Power movement with the ambitions of an emerging generation that sought to define their own being and system of beliefs.

The death of Tupac not only crushed the spirit of those in the hood who identified him as their Black messiah; Tupac's death also crushed the spirit of Biggie. By September 1996, my recording with Biggie and Shaq had been completed and delivered into the hands of T.W.Is.M./ Interscope Records. Biggie and I were deep in conversation about how I could turn a Minnie Riperton sample into a music composition Biggie intended to use for a song he was writing for Salt-N-Pepa. In fact, he asked me to consider co-producing several songs with him to reinvent the sound and style of the iconic rap group. In between the pitching of ideas through phone conversations, Biggie expressed that he was deeply hurt by the loss of his closest comrade, Tupac. Contrary to the opinion of many in the general public, Biggie never stopped loving his friend and anticipated the day when the conflict between the two would come to a close; he was confident that, when the moment presented itself, both parties would reconcile. Unfortunately, in March 1997, Biggie succumbed to a similar gunshot-related fate while exiting a party hosted by *Vibe* magazine at the Petersen Automotive Museum in Los Angeles. I was supposed to be at that promotional party. Our plans to produce new music for Salt-N-Pepa and Biggie's plans to add Clean Cut to the hip-hop group Junior M.A.F.I.A. were brought to a tragic standstill.

My historic record with Biggie would be brought back to life in 2001 when Michael Jackson hired Rodney Jerkins to produce the song "Unbreakable." Rodney was one of the very first to hear a rough edit of the song "Still Can't Stop the Reign" from my recording session with Shaq. Rodney sought permission to retrieve the vocals from my original recording to be used as a feature on Michael Jackson's hit single. Neither Biggie, Shaq, nor I ever thought that our creative efforts in Shaq's studio would ever grab the attention of arguably the greatest entertainer of all time. Shaq and Biggie had set out to proclaim that their reign would never end. Thanks to Rodney, Michael Jackson sealed their efforts with "Unbreakable."

## RISING ANEW

I proposed the idea that radically intrusive storms are quite common to the human experience. Sometimes these storms are experienced in a moment, sometimes as a series of distinct disruptions, sometimes as a result of our own moral failures or ill-informed decisions. Since I am a man of faith, I believe our sacred storms arise out of both the natural order and the spiritual realm. No matter how or where such storms arise, we need divine guidance to weather them. We need a transcendent power to teach us the valuable life lessons that arise out of our storms to prepare us for the journeys ahead.

Jesus ventured into the storm that arose on the Sea of Galilee to remind the disciples that God was with them even while he was aware it altered their trajectory. Jesus modeled for the disciples how compassionate servant-leadership ought to be demonstrated when faith wanes in the face of stormy weather. Jesus saw the disciples in distress, walked on water toward where they struggled, spoke into the wind, causing the storm to cease, and entered the boat with them. Jesus then rode with the disciples from the middle of the sea toward the shore of Gennesaret, where he moored the boat and disembarked with them. There, anyone who drew close to Jesus was healed, even by simply touching the edge of his clothing. With healing, they were granted the opportunity to live life anew.

Living life anew requires more than just a random reshaping of one's daily habits. To live anew is to live authentically in community. To live anew is to express what it means to be both fully human and divinely inspired. By fully human, I am referring to one's capacity to hold in tension the existential concerns of others while embracing one's role as a caring and compassionate being. Jesus gave an example of such compassion in the parable of the Good Samaritan (Luke 10:25–37). Dr. Martin Luther King, Jr. expounded upon the moral gravity associated with living authentically as a compassionate human being when he questioned the death-dealing policies of the Lyndon B. Johnson administration during the Vietnam War. According to King, to be authentically human and compassionate we must confront—and if need be deconstruct— those policies, practices, and attitudes perverting peace, justice, and fairness in any given society.[2] If we consider the existential concerns of our neighbor, we will work to transform our social institutions in such a way that our attitudes and behaviors will embody a collective pursuit for peace, equality, and justice for all, not only for the powerful and the privileged. If we fully recognize and embrace what makes each individual distinctly unique, we will work to create life-affirming rituals that reinforce our right to exist peacefully and reject those soul-crushing policies and behavioral patterns that divide us by gender, ethnicity, class, race, or political affiliation. This work of living life anew and affirming each other's humanity in a unified community, grounded in compassion, must be engaged by local groups large and small to foster a truer sense of belonging that can address particular needs and desires in real time.

By living divinely inspired, I am referring to the acknowledgement of a supernatural force beyond the self that compels one to live creatively and love more authentically. For the Christian, Jesus is the penultimate example of what it meant to live a divinely inspired life. By all accounts recorded in the four Gospels, Jesus adhered to a love ethic that inspired a deep devotion to God and fostered a commitment to recentering the poor, oppressed, and the marginalized in God's salvific plan. To live a divinely inspired life is to fulfill the greatest commandment: to love God with all one's heart, soul, and mind; to love one's neighbor as one loves oneself (Matthew 22:36–40). For the follower of Jesus, intentional and comprehensive devotion is the mark of an authentic, God-fearing

---

2. Martin Luther King Jr., "Beyond Vietnam: A Time to Break Silence," sermon, Riverside Church, New York City, April 4, 1967.

believer. However, one's intense devotion to God must be equally matched with one's intense devotion to one's neighbor if the believer is to truly live divinely inspired.

If we are living a divinely inspired life, we will interrogate the moral underpinnings of policies that cause bodily harm and death to the poor, powerless, and oppressed. If we are living a divinely inspired life, we will challenge belief systems that produce false social constructs that divide people-groups by skin color as a justification for systemic racism, mass incarceration, and capital gain. If we are to live a divinely inspired life, we will push back against hypocritical attitudes and hyperpatriarchal beliefs that normalize biased aggressions toward members of the LGBTQIA community and devalue the humanity of women. To be authentically Christian is to love God and to join in the work of expanding God's spiritual community, through which life options are made available to all. This work of neighborly love and justice is inspired by the teachings of Jesus and rooted in a deep devotion toward deconstructing the attitudes that take, rather than affirm, the lives of those created in God's image. This is the kind of work that accepts individuals as they are. It creates space for each member of society to find their authentic voice. The divinely inspired life embraces the motherless and the fatherless; it affirms the dreams and aspirations of the immigrant; it provides safe shelter for the homeless and displaced; it uplifts the poor, marginalized, and oppressed as equal members of what Dr. King defined as the beloved community.[3]

## TOWARD SOMETHING NEW

Our unexpected sacred storms are God's gift to us in the sense that they offer us the opportunity for a new beginning. In such beginnings, we are afforded the privilege of learning afresh what it means to be both fully human and fully reliant upon an all-merciful, at times mysterious,

---

3. Martin Luther King Jr., "The Birth of a New Nation," sermon, Dexter Avenue Baptist Church, Montgomery, AL, April 7, 1957.

omniscient God. With the word "Go," God radically disrupted Abram's life with a promissory call toward a new land, covenantal blessing, seed, family, and nation (Genesis 12:1–9). All that had taken place in Abram's life in the land of Haran prior to God's radically intrusive call served as a graceful prelude to the new life of blessing and covenant in the land of Canaan. Not every sacred storm is so gentle or promising at its outset. Storms can come in the form of a car burning down in front of the church, compelling a young mother to walk through the front door; in the form of a faithless husband abandoning a young mother with four children; in the form of a trauma-triggered emotional crisis that paralyzes a university student's forward movement toward graduation. There are the storms that show up in the form of prostate cancer, challenging the faith of a God-fearing man who loves to teach Sunday school and serves in the prison ministry.

In each instance, the individual heard the word "Go" and by faith chose to press through the storm with divine purpose and calling. The mother with the burning car has been a member of the church for more than thirty years and serves on the Board of Elders. The mother with four children has become an active participant in the ministries of her church. The university student who froze in fear during the middle of sophomore year of college has graduated. The Sunday school teacher and prison ministry advocate is now in full remission. Each one encountered an unexpected storm. Each one had their own particular set of pursuits, aspirations, and ambitions prior to the storm. Each one attested to an inner conviction that God was present with them in the midst of their storm. Each one ascribed to a new sense of purpose and life ambition after receiving comfort and encouragement to live life anew on the backside of their disruptive event.

There is little wonder that—on the backside of the assassinations of Malcolm X and Dr. Martin Luther King, Jr., a waning Black power movement, and Ronald Reagan's trickle-down voodoo economics—youth in the Bronx and surrounding boroughs began creating their own kind of cultural expressions. In place of the creative arts, music, and college prep programs that were slashed from the public schools of New York City, hip-hop culture emerged as an alternative community in which new interpretations of self-individualization and meaning came together to form a new sense of belonging. The MC (preacher), DJ (worship leader), break-dancer (liturgical artist), graffiti painter (scribe), and journalist (teacher of the law) took center stage in response to the corrosive politics that strangled the life out of Black and Brown communities throughout the five boroughs. Determined to live rather than die, Black genius learned to survive and thrive through the cultural expressions of DJ Kool Herc, the Sugar Hill Gang, Rock Steady Crew, Cornbread, Tracy 168, Fab 5 Freddy, and Lee Quiñones.

As the evolution of the linguistic genre called "rap" continued, rappers like Grandmaster Flash and the Furious Five, Kurtis Blow, Melle Mel, and the Cold Crush Brothers paved the way for rappers like Ice-T, LL Cool J, Roxanne Shanté, Brett B., Chuck D, KRS-One, Rakim, MC Lyte, Nas, Jay-Z, Queen Latifah, The Notorious B.I.G., Scarface, Will Smith, Snoop Dogg, Lil' Kim, N.W.A., Kendrick Lamar, Lauryn Hill, J. Cole, Cardi B, Drake, Lil Wayne, André 3000, and Migos. As the analogue-turned-digital genre dubbed "DJing" continued to evolve, disc jockeys like DJ Kool Herc, DJ Grand Wizard Theodore, and Grandmaster Flash begat converted DJs into music producers like Lovebug Starski, DJ Marley Marl, Hurby "Luv Bug" Azor, D-Moet, Dr. Dre, DJ Eddie F, Pete Rock, DJ Premier, Havoc, Easy Mo Bee, DJ Quik, Buckwild, DJ Muggs, Q-Tip, J Dilla, RZA, Just Blaze, Kanye West, Salaam Remi, Scott Storch, Hit-Boy, 9th Wonder, Zaytoven, Swizz Beats, Cardo, Mannie Fresh, Metro Boomin, and ATL Jacob. The story of hip-hop could be described as a story of perpetual evolution, in which radically disruptive moments in history created opportunities for a disenfranchised population to recenter itself as an empowered community in pursuit of meaning and, at times, a more transcendent purpose.

Much in the same way, the Black church in America evolved out of catastrophically disruptive moments in history, such as the abduction of three hundred eighty-eight thousand Africans from their homeland between the years 1526 and 1808.[4] None can dispute the fact that the Black church inspired death-defying acts of liberation and rebellion in the face of a chattel system aimed to destroy the souls of a stolen African people. The hope for a better present and future, cultivated in the Black church, empowered enslaved individuals who were determined to withstand torture and the suffocating denial of their humanity. This spiritual strength was cultivated in the Black church as much as it was cultivated through the practice of Islam, African humanism, and other forms of African traditional religion brought over with the imported slave population. Much like with the more recent evolutions of hip-hop, the Black church continues to foster distinct aspects of African American culture apart and away from the reach of those who would seek to destroy it. Historically speaking, the church served as the first formalized space where Black genius could be put on display, practiced and perfected, and expressed at one time and in one place. The Black church allowed for the creative expressions of music, dance, and song; rhetoric and oratory; poetry and prose; textual exegesis and interpretation; memorization, reading, and writing; the dramatic arts and scripting; call-and-response, signifying, and indirection; philosophizing and theorizing; thus, one cannot forget, "of course, mastering all 'the flowers of speech.'"[5]

What shall we say then about how faith is being and will be creatively expressed on the backside of a disruptive pandemic? I ask this question as a product of both hip-hop and the Black church, an embodiment of the many distinct cultural expressions and beliefs that make both communities particularly similar and yet extraordinarily different. Already, faith on the backside of a the COVID-19 storm has focused less on tradition and more on connection to God and neighbor. Faith compels the church to invest in digital spaces for such connections and cultivate partnerships outside the physical walls of the church. The church that

---

4. Henry Louis Gates Jr., *The Black Church: This Is Our Story, This Is Our Song* (New York: Penguin Press, 2021), 22.

5. Ibid., xxii.

has landed on the shores of Gennesaret will not deny a disciple's desire for connection just because of their infrequent physical presence; in faith the church will bear God's touch across multiple platforms. Creative faith suggests that the church must stretch towards those who seek connection with the hope that they will find a sense of belonging and experience evidence of Jesus within a spiritual community.

No matter the nature of one's system of beliefs or mode of gathering, love is the universal language that crosses over all cultural divides. As a Christian, I ascribe to the teachings of Jesus of Nazareth as the fullest embodiment of how the selfless love of God can be modeled on Earth. I also contend that the story of Mark 6:45–56 captures for believers and nonbelievers alike a wonderful example of how the love ethic of Jesus can be lived out in a world held captive by multiple storms. Much like the disciples whose journey to Bethsaida was thrown off course, our paths in search of love, meaning, happiness, progress, financial stability, and creative expression are often disrupted by sacred storms that land us on shores we never envisioned. As I mentioned earlier, my conversion experience in the Jersey City recording studio radically disrupted the path I had chosen for my own professional pursuits. Though we may be terrified and tossed about as the disciples were, I contend that such storms are sacred in the sense that God dwells with us in the midst of the unexpected. Therefore, we have hope despite our struggle with the unknown.

Modeling the compassionate character of God, when we have a genuine love and respect for our neighbor, we will meet them at their points of distress and deploy our resources, political power, and social influence to free the vulnerable from the storms engulfing their lives. As followers of Jesus, when we humble ourselves and allow Christ's character to be "seen" by those seeking an authentic encounter with God, the power of touch can transcend the limits of both quarantine and technology so that the healing power of God can be experienced by all.

Mark's Gospel teaches that the healing touch of Jesus gives access to a new beginning—a beginning in which the echoing pains and struggles of the past are quieted. I suggest the church will be at its best when it embodies the radical teachings of Jesus to the degree that it works to upend any social systems working against God's intent to give life more abundantly.

As the Black church builds upon the hard-fought advancements accomplished through the efforts of the civil rights, Black Power, and Black Lives Matter movements, it will need to refocus its gaze upon those systems and policies continuing to administer death upon the most fragile, marginalized, and othered in society. Its pulpits will need to remain committed to a prophetic homiletical tradition that speaks truth to power and dares to proclaim what Dr. Frank Thomas defined as dangerous sermons in order to upend the systemic evils that trap the vulnerable in its elaborate web.[6] The Black homiletic tradition will need to remain grounded in what Dr. Kenyatta Gilbert described as "daring speech," a methodology through which the preacher who preaches prophetically stands resolute while revealing God's transcendent truth in the face of sinful activities that frustrate God's life-giving purposes.[7] Not only must the church's message contain demon-crushing, yoke-breaking power, its worship experiences must point authentically to a God whose presence is near and whose power to heal is accessible to all those in search of spiritual renewal and restoration. Most importantly, the Black church must double its efforts not only to partner with justice-seeking coalitions advocating for the protection of voting rights, gun reform laws, affordable housing, cost-effective healthcare, and a quality public education system, but also to reengage in the work of supporting young entrepreneurs who can become the economic base of their local communities.

While it might be true that storms are disruptive and, when unexpected, can leave us in a state of paralysis, Mark 6:45–56 reminds us that we are not alone. God looks upon us with care and concern, always at the ready and waiting to step in and remind us that not even

6. Frank A. Thomas, *How to Preach a Dangerous Sermon* (Nashville: Abingdon, 2018).
7. Kenyatta Gilbert, *Exodus Preaching: Crafting Sermons About Justice and Hope* (Nashville: Abingdon, 2018).

life's turbulent winds can separate us from God's unending love. Not only does God step in with us, God journeys with us toward a new destination where we get to see God's redemptive purpose usher in the manifestation of healing and renewal for those in search of a new beginning.

## NEW PATHS AND NEW WINDS LEADING FORWARD

Several weeks after pondering Shirley Bell's official invitation to be managed by Flavor Unit Management, I agreed to join the Flavor Unit family. Beginning in October 1996, all inquiries from record labels and recording artists were filtered through Shirley. Not long after my official commitment, Shirley suggested that I travel to the home of Naughty By Nature's Grammy-Award-winning producer Kay Gee in New Jersey. The plan was to play music tracks for Kay Gee in the hope that he would consider selecting a few of my compositions for Naughty By Nature's next album. At Kay Gee's studio, Kay Gee presented himself as the consummate professional and introduced me to all of the individuals with us in his listening room. I proceeded to turn over my DAT, which contained roughly ten to twelve instrumentals. The songs were structured in such a way that the listener would experience a methodical building up— much in the way that church goers experience the crescendo at the close of Black preaching. While the structure of the DAT made the emotional effect I intended, Kay Gee did not commit to any of the tracks submitted. I could understand: Naughty By Nature was known for their melodic anthems, whereas I constructed a series of much edgier tracks that would have appealed to a different audience at that time.

In February 1997, I returned to Madison Square Garden for the first time since the Source Awards in 1995. I had been invited to attend the 39th Annual Grammy Awards to be introduced to record company executives soliciting musical tracks for the upcoming soundtrack to the movie *Soul Food*. Having already contributed to the *Panther* and *Bad Boys* movie soundtracks, it was suggested that I would be a lock to produce at least one track on the album. As performers like Chaka Khan, Bruce

Springsteen, Tracy Chapman, the Fugees, Mary J. Blige, Whitney Houston, and Brandy graced the Grammy stage with stellar performances, I felt the wind blowing again. This was the same wind that preceded the one who visited me in my studio in December 1996. He did not reappear while I sat at the Grammy Awards, but his presence was felt. I began to discern that the stage in front of me would no longer be the stage I aimed to pursue. Without saying a word, I rose from my VIP seating and left the facility. As I walked onto 33rd Street, the wind subsided. It was time to follow a path that had been selected for me rather than choose a path of my own. Within thirty days, I informed Shirley Bell and those with whom I had a contractual relationship that, at the conclusion of the recordings I had committed myself to, I would follow the lead of the one who visited me several months before.

I am often asked, "How could you possibly walk away from an industry where you had become so successful so quickly? How does one walk away from a career that barely started? Do you regret leaving behind the opportunity to create generational wealth for yourself and your family?"

My response has always been that, while I may have less materially in this season of my life, I have so much more love, joy, and peace of mind. When I first walked away from the money and the fame, I often questioned my decision. I no longer do so. It remains debatable whether I was functioning in my divine calling when I expressed myself creatively as a music producer; I am certain that I am functioning in my divine calling and purpose now. As a person of faith, I am convinced that the only reason one would leave behind the unique experiences and lifestyle I was afforded, prior to my conversion as a follower of Jesus, was if they had been radically disrupted by a sacred storm.

My favorite professor of religion at Rutgers University, Dr. Mahlon H. Smith III, would often say to his students, "If you were among the original group of disciples in Galilee, you would have to be crazy to follow Jesus after his crucifixion. You did so knowing that you would suffer the same fate Jesus did at Calvary. The disciples did so anyway. Why?" After pausing for twenty seconds or so, Dr. Smith would drop the anvil of an answer: "My dear brothers and sisters, I will tell you why. I am convinced that they saw something. They saw something so powerful and significant that it turned their lives upside down." Dr. Smith's answer is the very same that I offer to all inquirers today. I saw something. I saw something so powerful and radically disruptive that it literally turned my life upside down.